Western Press Coverage of News in the Third World

Western Press Coverage of News in the Third World

A Bibliographical Review of Literature (1976–1988)

Sunny Tszesun Li

The Chinese University Press

ISBN 962–201–532–8

THE CHINESE UNIVERSITY PRESS
The Chinese University of Hong Kong
SHATIN, N.T., HONG KONG

Printed in Hong Kong by Nam Fung Printing Co., Ltd.

Contents

Preface

This book comprises three parts: (1) journal articles (including trade journals and magazines); (2) books, book chapters, monographs, papers and reports; and (3) doctoral dissertations and master's theses. All entries are arranged alphabetically and chronologically from 1988 to 1976. Overall, 203 items have been included: 101 items for Part I, 57 for Part II and 45 for Part III.

The purpose of this book is twofold: (1) To serve as a research resource, i.e. a tool in the area of international communication, especially on the topic of Western press coverage of the Third World. It is particularly useful in forming research ideas and in evaluating research on topics related to the flow and coverage of foreign news. (2) To serve as a reference in a course such as International Communication at both the undergraduate and graduate levels, so that students can have a multiplicity of choices as to what they are interested in reading.

Though the title of this book is not difficult to comprehend, a brief explanation might help. The "Western press" refers primarily to the print media (including the international news agencies) from North America, Western Europe and Australia, particularly those from the United States of America. The "Third World" is simply a convenient term for developing countries throughout the world, including those in Asia, Latin America, Africa and the Middle East.* Several terms with the same reference have

---

* For coding purposes, Schramm and Atwood adopted this definition for the Third World in *Circulation of News in the Third World—A Study of Asia*: (1) all Asian states except Japan and the Asian part of the USSR; (2) all Pacific states except Australia and New Zealand; (3) all Latin American states except Argentina; (4) all African states except South Africa; (5) all Middle East states except Israel; (6) no European states—either East or West Europe—except Albania; (7) no states of North America. I would exclude any part of the Soviet Union but include Argentina in the Third World. Appendix III has included 155 countries and territories on the Third World list.

been used in academia: "Third World countries", "less developed countries", "advancing countries" and "developing countries". The year of 1976 was chosen simply because it was in that year that developing countries first used the term "New International Information Order" (NIIO) in the Non-Aligned Symposium of Information held in Tunisia.

This compilation carries two foci—one major and the other secondary. The major focus deals with content analyses of the Western press coverage of specific events and issues in the Third World. The secondary focus concerns concepts and issues surrounding the debate of the NIIO, including problems pertinent to news flow in the Third World and foreign correspondents' gathering and reporting of Third World news. Inherent in these two foci are two broad theoretical dichotomies. First, the distinction between Western-style "objective" journalism and "critical" or "advocacy" journalism often associated with Marxist views and espoused by many developing countries. Second, the distinction between information hegemony sustained by the established Western media and the call for a more pluralist and democratic information order advocated by many Third World scholars and representatives. In addition, this book includes, to a lesser extent, the Western press coverage of UNESCO activities related to international communication issues and some reflective pieces written by professional journalists about the problems in Third World coverage. The scope of some entries is very broad but some aspects of them are so appropriate for this topic that they really deserve to be included and have been included by the compiler.

Sunny Tszesun Li
October, 1991
The Chinese University of Hong Kong

Acknowledgements

This bibliography is primarily the result of the literature review and independent study undertaken with Professor Robert Kamm, former president of the Oklahoma State University (OSU), where I was a doctoral student working on the dissertation. Besides Professor Kamm, one of my advisers who inspired me to serious academic work, I would like to take this opportunity to thank Dr. Marlan Nelson, Director of the OSU School of Journalism and Broadcasting, who allowed me to use the School library at my discretion.

Thanks are also due to the Interlibrary Loan Service of Edmon Low Library, which asked so many U.S. libraries for help on my behalf; and to Dr. Russell G. Todd, professor of the University of Hong Kong, who gave me advice on the Preface during the last stage of preparing this manuscript in Hong Kong. I also wish to thank Mr. T. L. Tsim, Director, and the editorial and production staff of The Chinese University Press for their kind assistance. And the last but not the least, gratitude should go to my wife, Ivy Lo, for sharing not only the household but also clerical work; and to my daughters Amy Zhao-li and Annabelle Jerry, for their spiritual support. Without the sincere help of all these people, it would not have been possible for me to complete this book on this date.

Abbreviations

ABC (American Broadcasting Company)
AFP (Agence France-Presse)
ANPA (American Newspaper Publishers Association)
AP (The Associated Press)
ASEAN (Association of Southeast Asian Nations)
ASNE (American Society of Newspaper Editors)
BBC (British Broadcasting Corporation)
CANA (Caribbean News Agency)
CBS (Columbia Broadcasting System)
CCAS (Centre for Contemporary Arab Studies)
CCCP (The Central Committee of the Communist Party)
CP (Canadian Press)
FBIS (Foreign Broadcast Information Service)
GIN (Global Information Network)
GNA (Gulf News Agency)
GNP (Gross National Product)
IAMCR (International Association for Mass Communication Research)
IPDC (International Programme for the Development of Communication)
IPS (Inter Press Service)
KAL (Korean Airlines)
KUNA (Kuwait News Agency)
NANAP (Non-Aligned News Agencies Pool)
NBC (National Broadcasting Company)
NCNA (New China News Agency)
NFLA (National Front for the Liberation of Angola)
NIEO (New International Economic Order)
NIICO (New International Information and Communication Order)
NIIO (New International Information Order)
NUTIA (National Union for the Total Independence of Angola)
NWICO (New World Information and Communication Order)
NWIO (New World Information Order)
OIIO (Old International Information Order)

OPEC (Organization of Petroleum Exporting Countries)
PLO (Palestine Liberation Organization)
PMLA (Popular Movement for the Liberation of Angola)
PRC (People's Republic of China)
ROC (Republic of China)
SASO (South African Students' Organization)
TWA (Trans World Airlines)
TWIN (Third World Information Network)
TWNA (Third World News Agency)
UK (United Kingdom)
UN (United Nations)
UNESCO (United Nations Educational, Scientific and Cultural Organiza-
    tion)
UPI (United Press International)
USSR (Union of Soviet Socialist Republics)
VOA (Voice of America)
WEIS (World Event Interaction Survey)

Part I

Journal Articles

1.

Barranco, Deborah A. and Leonard Shyles. Spring 1988. "Arab vs. Israeli News Coverage in *The New York Times*, 1976 and 1984." *Journalism Quarterly*, 65(1):178–81.

> The authors examined "aggrandizement" bias in *The New York Times'* Middle East coverage by comparing coverage of events, issues and leaders of Israel and America with those from 10 prominent Arab nations: Egypt, Syria, Libya, Iraq, Saudi Arabia, Lebanon, Palestine/PLO, Sudan, Jordan and Kuwait. Two major analyses were conducted. First, a "Headline Proper Mention" measure was used to examine the frequency of each country's appearance in the headline. Results show that the frequencies of proper mention attributed to Israel and the U.S. were significantly greater than those attributed to Arab nations both in 1976 and 1984. Second, results of the analysis of the "Primary and Secondary Focus Nation" indicated that Israel and the U.S. were indeed mentioned significantly more frequently.

2.

Chang, Tsan-kuo. Summer 1988. "The News and U.S.–China Policy: Symbols in Newspapers and Documents." *Journalism Quarterly*, 65(2):320–27.

> The purpose of the study is to determine if political symbols in United States newspaper reporting between 1950 and 1984 reflected official U.S. policies toward China. The author analysed government documents and front page news in *The New York Times* and *The Washington Post*. The paragraph was used as the coding unit. Ideological, geographical and legal symbols were analysed. China policy news was defined as "news and opinions regarding U.S. relations with both the People's Republic of China and the Republic of China. It was found that symbolic emphasis shifted from abstract ideological and emotional symbols to more precise symbols, and the change in symbols emphasis paralleled changes in U.S. policy, as relations with China improved during the 1970s and early 1980s. The author concluded that the symbols used by leading U.S. newspapers to represent the "two Chinas" closely reflected U.S. policy toward those countries.

3.

Sumser, John. Fall 1987. "Labels Used to Define Central American Situation." *Journalism Quarterly*, 64(3):850–53.

The author examined key concepts in news coverage of events in Nicaragua and El Salvador to test the idea that the conceptual framework used by the news media helps create and maintain a picture of the world in accordance with the views and values of America's ruling elite. The sample includes all articles in the first section of *The New York Times* and *New York Post* from 1983 with headlines referring to Central America or any Central American country. Key concepts including words such as guerrilla, soldier, government, clique, leftist, left, and right, were examined. Results indicated that one government, Nicaragua, is consistently depreciated, dismissed as a political party which is under attack by "rebels" and lacks the ability to protect itself. El Salvador, on the other hand, is never called a political faction or party, but rather is defined as a nation or government with a competent military capability of turning back the "guerrillas."

4.

Ogan, Christine. Spring 1987. "Coverage of Development News in Developed and Developing Countries." *Journalism Quarterly*, 64(1):80–87.

The author analysed the coverage of the United Nations and International Conference on Population in Mexico from 4–14 August 1984 in a number of newspapers and magazines in the U.S., Western Europe,* Africa and Latin America to determine if reporters covered the Conference more as a political event than a development event and to examine the degree of discretionary latitude the reporters used in covering the event. It was found that newspapers and news magazines in developed countries were more likely to cover the political issues raised at the Conference and less on population issues. Reporters from developing countries tended to rely soly on government sources more often than those from developed countries. Stories from developing countries were less in depth and included little analysis, while those from developed countries were longer. In both countries, reporters wrote minimally about official speeches, and cited speakers in low proportion to the total number of sources, which indicates reporters had great latitude in reporting the Conference.

* The Western press in this study refers to: *Irish Times* (Ireland), *The Times* (London), *Le Monde* and *Le Figaro* (France), *The Globe and Mail* (Toronto), *The London Free Press* (Canada), *The New York Times, Chicago Tribune, Los Angeles Times* and *The Christian Science Monitor* (U.S.). Western magazines from developed countries are: *L'Express, Le Nouvel Observateur* and *Actuel Developpement* (France), *Macleans Canada's Weekly Newsmagazine, Newsweek* and *Time* (U.S.).

5.

Potters, W. James. Spring 1987. "News from Three Worlds in Prestige U.S. Newspapers." *Journalism Quarterly*, 64(1):73–79.

The author examined front page international news with headlines two or more inches of copy in eight U.S. newspapers* in 1913, 1933, 1963, and 1983. Nations covered were considered either Eastern, Western, or the Third World. Results showed that international news occupied 43.6% of the total sample. The West dominated the coverage, with 72.6% of items dealing with only Western nations. Including items coded in more than one category, Third World nations were covered in 20.6% of international news items. Coverage involving the Third World shifted from 15.9% of international news in 1913 to 10% in 1933, 24.5% in 1963 and 40.9% in 1983.

* The eight U.S. newspapers are: *The New York Times, The Washington Post, Chicago Tribune, St. Louis Post-Dispatch, The Atlanta Constitution, The Miami Herald, Los Angeles Times,* and *The Christian Science Monitor.*

6.

Ramaprasad, Jyotika and Daniel Riffe. Summer/Autumn 1987. "Effect of U.S.–Indian Relations on *New York Times* Coverage." *Journalism Quarterly*, 64(2):537–43.

The authors analysed *The New York Times*, U.S. Department of State Bulletins and congressional publications to examine relationships between U.S. newspaper coverage of India and U.S. foreign policy toward India between 1973 and 1980. The authors constructed one sample week per month for the study. The prominence of items and the emphasis within items (favourable, neutral, unfavourable) were considered. Results showed fewer items occurred during the Carter Administration. Items with an unfavourable emphasis were less common, and those with a neutral emphasis were more common, during those four years, than during other years (items with a favourable emphasis were equally common throughout the study). The authors concluded that changes in mean length and prominence scores of items on India in the *Times* over the policy periods were not significant and did not parallel U.S. foreign policy toward India.

7.

Alrabaa, S. 1986. "Western Mass Media Hegemony Over the Third World." *Communications: The European Journal of Communication*, 12(1):7–20.

The author argues that international mass media are primarily dominated by major Western power centres. Unidirectionality—a one-way flow of news and information from the West to the Third World—characterizes the content, standards, and criteria of these media. This implies a major cultural influence of the West in terms of socialization, ideological control and imbalance of power between the West and other parts of the world. The author rejects the modernization theories which advocate the vitality of modern mass media for developing the Third World, and argues that the efforts to convert the Third World into a replica of the First World serve mainly the domestic marketing need of the West. Western media hegemony, he says, reinforces existing unequal economic and political relations between producers in the West and consumers in the developing world.

8.

Gaddy, Gary D. and Enoh Tanjong. Spring 1986. "Earthquake Coverage by the Western Press."* *Journal of Communication*, 36(2):105–109.

The authors argue that news bias can be established only when there exist an appropriate basis of comparison and an objective determination of reality. It is not sufficient for Third World critics to conclude that

Western coverage of news in the Third World is biased provided that they can demonstrate that the news of other regions is not also uniformly biased (negative) and that the events occurring in the Third World are not in reality more negative than those occurring in the First World. With these assumptions, they recorded the geographical origin as well as human and physical consequences of more than 100 earthquakes and analysed their coverage. They found 71% of all earthquake reports from the Third World; however, 65% of all earthquakes of geographical significance also occurred in the Third World. Thus they concluded that Western media's coverage of earthquakes is not determined by geographical origin, but by human and physical consequences.

* The Western press refers to: *The New York Times*, *The Times* (London), and three major U.S. television networks: ABC, CBS and NBC.

9.

Hassan, A. M. 1986. "Some Problems of News Gathering and News Dissemination in Countries of Asia." *Media Asia*, 13(2):76–78.

The author points out three factors related to gathering and distributing news and information in Asia: (1) lopsided infrastructure with the industrialized and commercial sectors enjoying the latest technological innovations; (2) policies that consist of laws and regulations that restrict the gathering and interpretation of news; and (3) resources, which entail high operational costs.

10.

Kent, Thomas J. R. April 1986. "Foreign Reporting Demands Patience and Quick Wits in Addition to Good Journalism." *Presstime*, p. 42.

Kent, an experienced foreign correspondent, talks about how the job of the foreign correspondent has changed in the past few decades. Not only does it require more in-depth reporting within a meaningful context, but it also requires the access to information that has become more restricted despite the advancement of technology. Furthermore, its entry requirements have become much more competitive.

11.

Lubis, M. 1986. "Cultural Integrity: Free and Balanced Information

Flow—Mutually Exclusive Terms or Parts of the Same Thing?" *Media Asia*, 13(2):63–70.

Developing countries fear that their participation in the global information flow will threaten the integrity of their cultures. The author uses the example of Japan as a country that has successfully borrowed from other cultures and yet maintained its essential cultural elements, and recommends four major points for developing countries to achieve cultural integrity: (1) Every nation should carefully identify the positive values in its traditional culture. (2) Developing countries must foster their cultural capacity to adopt, adapt, and digest modern science. (3) Developing countries must begin to remedy their economic inequities as a prelude to participation in a "new" world information order. (4) Developing countries must develop a viable education system that incorporates the positive values of their countries' cultural heritage.

12.

Ruth, Marcia. April 1986. "Covering Foreign News." *Presstime*, pp. 28–35.

Ruth introduces changes in recent years in the coverage of foreign news by the Western news agencies and the press. Going beyond "coups-and-earthquakes" reporting, newspapers and the wires services are using various approaches to increase the breadth and depth of their foreign coverage. Foreign correspondents are producing in-depth reports that tell not only what happened but also what an international event means to the American reader. In addition, the focus of attention (as seen from the distribution of U.S. foreign correspondents) has shifted from Europe to the Third World, especially Latin America. The article includes a survey that shows a decline in the European presence from 54% to 31%, while in Latin America it increases from 10% to 23%; in Africa it increases from only a "token" presence to 8%, in the Middle East from 8% to 12%.

13.

Soderlund, Walter C. and Carmen Schmitt. Summer 1986. "El Salvador's Civil War as Seen in North and South American Press." *Journalism Quarterly*, 63(2):268–74.

The authors content analysed press coverage of El Salvador in major dailies of Argentina, Chile, Canada, and the U.S.* over a ten-week period in the fall of 1986. The analysis produced a data set of 160 news items dealing with El Salvador, broken down nearly equally between those appearing in the South American papers and those in the North American papers. Argentine papers led Chilean papers in coverage 42 stories to 36, while American papers led the Canadian papers 55 stories to 27. In general, the South American papers portrayed the Salvadorean junta, and especially the U.S., positively, while critical of the leftist factions in El Salvador, Cuba, and Nicaragua. North American papers, on the other hand, were negative to the performance of the junta and more positive to the leftist factions. Argentine and Chilean press had different patterns in the use of American or European wire services. Canadian and American press also differed, with the heavily America-originated Canadian information balanced by local staff writers.

* The North and South American dailies are *The Globe and Mail* (Toronto), *Ottawa Citizen*, *The New York Times*, *The Washington Post*, *La Nación* and *La Prensa* (both Argentina), *El Mercurio* and *La Tercera de la Hora* (both Chile).

14.

Aggarwala, Narinder K. 1985. "NIIO: A Hope or a Nightmare?" *Media Asia*, 12(1):44–53.

The New International Information Order (NIIO)* is a broad concept that refers to a process of global information flow as much as to a concrete entity. The genesis of the NIIO lies in the Third World leaders' perceptions of international news as predominantly Western. Aggarwala argues that there is considerable justification for the NIIO. Although it is criticized by the West as an unacceptable interference with the free flow of information, international news flows are not as objective, unbiased, or free as critics of NIIO and UNESCO** maintain. The challenge of the NIIO, he says, is to find a way to improve, strengthen, and expand information institutions and structures in the Third World so that the people of the developing countries, along with those in the industrialized world, become beneficiaries and not victims of the information technology revolution.

* The NIIO has been termed in various ways: the "New World Information Order",

"New International Information and Communication Order", and "New More Just and Efficient World Information and Communication Order". The NIIO debate involves developing countries in the Third World and developed countries in the Western world (the U.S. in particular). Being accused of imbalanced and biased reporting of the Third World, Western media respond by either refuting the charges on the basis of empirical evidence or counterattacking the proponents of the NIIO as plotting to curb the free flow of information.

** United Nations Educational, Scientific and Cultural Organization (UNESCO) was founded in 1946 "for the purpose of advancing, through the educational, scientific and cultural relations of the peoples of the world, the objectives of international peace and the common welfare of mankind". It has 164 members from all over the world.

15.

Chu, Leonard L. 1985. "An Organizational Perspective on International News Flow: Some Generalizations, Hypotheses, and Questions for Research." *Gazette*, 35(1):3–18.

The purpose of study is to identify the key problems in the news production process so that practical solutions can be worked out. Suggesting a "middle-of-the-road" approach to the international news flow in terms of the news production process which characterizes media organizations in both Western and Third World countries, Chu argues that the imbalance and unidirectionality in international news flow is inevitable, and certainly not conspiratory. Both Western and Eastern news media are constrained by organizational factors from providing the world with a truly objective or balanced view of reality. For Western media, the constraints are those of commercialism; for the Third World, the constraints are those of politics. The question is not a categorical "either-or" but a reorientation and rebalance of organizational values, priorities, and goals.

16.

Gulogulo, R. V. 1985. "Formal Obstacles to News Flow in Asia." *Media Asia*, 12(3):135–46.

This article reviews the information available on government actions, laws, and legal statutes that present obstacles to news flow in 13 Asian countries. The author identified three levels of news flow in Asia—news flow within the country, outside the country, and between Asian countries and the rest of the world. There are several types of restrictions: (1) obstacles from government regulations to news flow within the country; (2) obstacles from existing laws and legal statutes to news flow within the country; (3) obstacles from government regulations to news flow coming from outside the country or going out of the country; (4) obstacles from government regulations from existing laws and legal statutes to news flow between Asian countries; and (5) obstacles from existing laws and legal statutes to news flow between Asian countries.

17.

Hachten, William A. and Brian Beil. Fall 1985. "Bad News or No News? Covering Africa 1965–1982." *Journalism Quarterly*, 62(3):626–30.

This study intends to find out if coverage of Ghana and Tanzania in *The New York Times*, *The Times* (London), and *Milwaukee Journal* had changed since the early post-independence years. It was found that both the frequency and volume of coverage by the three newspapers had declined dramatically since 1965. The study did not support the argument that Western papers limit their coverage of developing countries to crisis events. (Only about 40% of 365 articles examined are crisis-oriented.) A reason is that as a result of fear of expulsion, Western journalists throughout the Third World adopted heavy self-censorship as a standard feature of reporting, especially in Africa. Consequently, the authors argue readers of Western papers are not receiving adequate information regarding the severe economic crisis and other problems facing the developing countries.

18.

Kirat, Mohamed and David Weaver. 1985. "Foreign News Coverage in Three Wire Services: A Study of AP, UPI, and the Non-Aligned News Agencies Pool." *Gazette*, 35(1):31–47.

Kirat and Weaver adopt the content analysis protocal devised for a multinational study of news flow conducted by the International Association for Mass Communication Research (IAMCR)* under the auspices of UNESCO. They coded a sample of 378 stories from January and February 1983. It was found that the less developed countries as a bloc are covered by the AP and UPI regional wire services as frequently as the more developed countries. The length of news stories about less developed and developed countries was roughly the same; the primary emphasis was on diplomatic and political activity, internal and armed conflicts, and crime. Economic and social issues, ecology, and medical/scientific topics were all neglected by coverage of both less and more developed countries. Contrary to the results of previous studies, however, there was a dramatic decline in the proportion of conflict or crisis news, especially in the Third World. This implies, the authors added, that the criticisms of the advocate of the New International Information Order (NIIO) may have had an impact on the news values of foreign correspondents and editors at wire services.

* At the end of his dissertation on which this article is based, the author has appended the IAMCR coding system, a list of developed and developing countries, and background information of the Non-Aligned News Agencies Pool (NANAP). The NANAP is an organization of information exchange that developing countries decided to establish in the non-aligned countries' summit meeting held in 1976. There were 86 countries willing to receive information from the NANAP in order to check the imbalance of international information flow.

19.

Menson, V. 1985. "Information Flow in Asia—An Overview." *Media Asia*, 12(2):63–56.

This article deals with information imbalance in Asia. The author concludes: (1) Co-operation and collective action have contributed to the growth of news agencies in Asia, but Western news agencies still dominate news transmission. (2) One reason for this continued dominance is the reluctance of Asian governments to lower tariffs and to facilitate investment in new technology. (3) The editorial judgement in Asia tends to favour transnational news sources, for reasons of quality, objectivity and immediacy. (4) By catching up with technological advances, the educational system is vital in facilitating information flow. (5) The technological gap is not a major problem, as examples in Hong Kong, Singapore and Malaysia have shown.

20.

Morris, Roger. January/February 1985. "Mexico: The U.S. Press Takes a Siesta." *Columbia Journalism Review*, pp. 31–36.

The author points out that the foreign press (Canadian, British and European) often does a better job than the U.S. press in covering Mexico's big problems. The U.S. coverage of its big neighbour's big problems such as corruption, agricultural failure, or repression lacks sophistication and meaningful context. Given the enormous U.S. stake in Mexico, the need for better Mexican coverage is overwhelming.

21.

Rahim, Syed A. 1985. "Understanding Cultural Problems in Transnational Information Flow." *Media Asia*, 12(2):80–87.

The author examines Schramm and Atwood's *Circulation of News in the Third World—A Study of Asia* as a means of establishing a case for a cultural approach to the study of information flow. He says Schramm and Atwood ignored at least one cultural variable, i.e. language. Discourse analyses, he proposes, provide powerful tools for examining news flow structures and interpreting the play of cultural factors in news flow processes. A discourse analysis should include both the textual and the contextual aspects of news flow.

22.

Soderlund, Walter C. Winter 1985. "Press Reporting on El Salvador and Nicaragua in Leading Canadian and American Newspapers." *Canadian Journal of Communication*, 11(4):353–68.

Soderlund analysed a sample of 25 issues each of *The Globe and Mail* (Toronto), *The New York Times*, *Ottawa Citizen* and *The Washington Post* from October 1983 to mid-December 1984 on an every-three-day basis. He examined all material on Central America by area of paper: front page, inside page, news, editorial, feature, and letters to the editor. It was found that events in Nicaragua and El Salvador accounted for 53.2% and 46.8% respectively of total items on Central America. American papers covered both Nicaragua and El Salvador far more than

Canadian papers. Hard news dominated coverage from both countries. *The New York Times* was the only paper that presented more items on El Salvador than on Nicaragua.

23.

Chu, James. 1984. "The Gathering of News about China." *Gazette*, 33(2):87–106.

This study examined how foreign journalists gather news about the People's Republic of China, their sources of information, the restrictions imposed upon them, the facilities provided by the Chinese government for the pursuit of their journalistic activities and what the foreign journalists consider newsworthy. The period of study extended from 1949 to 1963, and the main sources for the study were interviews, news stories, articles and books written by the foreign journalists in China. The author concluded that newsgathering conditions have been improved slowly in China where there is no overt censorship; however, the foreign correspondent uses translated articles from censored newspapers at the central level as a major source of information. The author argues this process places those Chinese newsmen in a significant gatekeeping position and the situation is strengthened by the unavailability of provincial and local newspapers to the correspondent.

24.

Giffard, C. Anthony. Spring 1984. "Developed and Developing Nation News in U.S. Wire Service Files to Asia." *Journalism Quarterly*, 61(1):14–19.

Giffard analysed AP and UPI Asia wire service copy drawn from a six-week period in 1980. The sample comprises a constructed week of 7 randomly selected days with a total of 1,009 news reports, 556 from AP and 453 from UPI. It was found that there was more Asian news on the Asian wire services of the two American agencies than news of any other region. Among developing countries, China, Iran and Thailand topped the list, each occupying more than 8% of the composite news. Third World countires such as Angola, Ethiopia, Morocco, Cuba, Jaimaca, Nicaragua, Ecuador, Paraguay, Burma, Lebanon, Nepal, Nigeria, Sierra

Leone (a small country in West Africa), each occupying 0.3%. While the proportion of reports from developing countries as a whole was only one-third of the total, the absolute number was substantial. Reports from the developing countries were, on average, longer than those from the developed countries, contradicting the notion that Third World events are covered only sketchily in comparison to those of the West. Politics or military matters comprised the bulk of the reportage, with comparatively little attention devoted to social services, religion, culture or science in the Third World.

25.

Haule, John James. 1984. "International Press Coverage of African Events: The Delemma and the Future." *Gazette*, 33(2):107–14.

Haule maintained that independent countries of Southern Africa have to take measures to uphold their sovereignty in light of South Africa's declared sustained efforts to destabilize them. At the same time the decision of these states to ban South African-based correspondents has been seized upon by the opponents of the New International Information Order as another manifestation of the Third World alleged desire to restrict the right of access of Western news media to cover events in developing countries. In this article, the author selectively analysed Western media* coverage of a nationwide speech by President Julius Nyerere of Tanzania to illustrate the dilemma which developing countries face at the hands of Western media. He also discussed the structural and theoretical explanations of international news flow, and explored ways by which African states can get better coverage from the international news media.

* The author conducted a computer search of the news event in the Western press. He found that the event was reported by *The Times* (London), but many major British newspapers—*Daily Telegraph, Daily Mail, Daily Express, Daily Mirror, Financial Times, Evening Standard, The Guardian* (Manchester), *The Observer, Sunday Express, Sunday Telegraph* and the *Sunday Times*—did not cover it. Nor did many leading U.S. dailies—*The New York Times, Los Angeles Times, The Boston Globe, The Christian Science Monitor* and *The Washington Post*. Although the BBC, the VOA, the AP and Reuters also reported the event, the daily newspapers in Tanzania's neighbouring countries of Kenya, Uganda, Moszambique and Malawi did not report it.

26.

Lent, John A. 1984. "To and From the Grave: Press Freedom in South Asia." *Gazette*, 33(1):17–36.

The author surveyed press freedom in Afghanistan, Bangladesh, Nepal, Pakistan and Sri Lanka and concluded that the prospects for an independent and free press in South Asia are not optimistic. The most frightening prospect is that the press will self-censor to the extent that the governments will not have to become very involved and that is more damaging in the long run than direct government control.

27.

Nordenstreng, Kaarle. Winter 1984. "Bitter Lessons: The 'World of the News' Study." *Journal of Communication*, 34(1):138–42.

The author, who initiated the idea and wrote the draft resolution of the "World of the News" study,* argued that the study is a simple, contemporary measurement of media performance devoid of "the changing economic and political relations in the international community." He said since the result of the study has been given a false interpretation in support of those who opposed the idea of a New International Information Order, the greatest impact of the study may have been in demonstrating the scientific inadequacy and political risks involved in one-sided quantitative consideration of mass media content.

* The "World of the News" study sponsored by UNESCO/IAMCR was carried out in 29 countries. In the context of the New International Information Order debate, the research project started under the title of "Foreign Images" study and was published as *Foreign News in the Media*. The Western newspapers involved were: six from the U.S. (*The New York Times*, *The Washington Post*, *Los Angeles Times*, *New York Daily News*, *Minneapolis Tribune* and *Charlotte Observer*), five from the Federal Republic of Germany (*Bild Zeitung*, *Die Welt*, *Frankfurter Allgemeine Zeitung*, *Süddeutscher Zeitung* and *Frankfurter Rundschau*), three from Australia (*The Australian*, *The Herald* and *Daily Telegraph*), three from the Netherlands (*Del Telegraaf*, *NRC-Handelsblad* and *Dagblad Tubantia*), four from Finland (*Helsingin Sanomat*, *Aamulehti*, *Kansan Uutiset* and *Savon Sanomat*), and one from Greece (*Ta Nea*).

28.

Samarajiwa, R. April 1984. "Third World Entry to the World Market in News: Problems and Possible Solutions." *Media, Culture and Society*, 6(2):119–36.

Recognizing the fact that news is a commodity in world markets, the author saw the worldwide production and distribution of news as a political-economic process. The Transnational News Agencies (TNA) were viewed primarily as firms that mobilize resources for the production and distribution of this commodity in economic markets. Considerations of profit seeking and market control were held to be as relevant to the analysis of TNA as they were to other business firms. Grounding the analysis in an account of actual market dynamics, and informed by a critique of the Western rhetoric of "free flow" of information, the author proposed a strategy for the production of more equitable news flows and argued that alterantive news production practices can only be developed out of a close and detailed analysis of the actual practice of capitalist markets in cultural commodities. He added a key element in formulating policies to restructure the market must be an awareness of the strengths and weaknesses of the dominant TNA and the Third World countries that challenge the domination.

29.

Sreberny-Mohammadi, Annabelle. Winter 1984. "The 'World of the News' Study: Results of International Co-operation." *Journal of Communication*, 34(1):121–33.

This article discusses the UNESCO/IAMCR-sponsored report on an international study of news coverage by press, radio and television in 29 press systems.* The author analysed all general news pages of the press: the news item was the unit of analysis, and each item was coded as to location, position, and nationality of action, topic, and theme. It was found that despite the diversity of systems, the structure of international news coverage was quite similar across systems. Politics dominated international news reporting everywhere. This was particularly true of the news media of the Southern hemisphere, where few "soft" stories of any type were generated. The other overall finding was the prominence of regionalism. Every national system devoted most attention to events happening within and to persons belonging to its immediate geographical region.

* See the note in Entry No. 27. Also see Entry No. 112.

30.

Stevenson, Robert L. Winter 1984. "Pseudo Debate." *Journal of Communication*, 34(1):134–38.

Stevenson, a member of the American team that participated in the analysis of the UNESCO/IAMCR-sponsored the "World of the News" study, first discussed the study's findings on the question of the influence of the Western news agencies' coverage of international news. He then examined whether the results of the study support the contention that mass media in the Third World are maintained in a state of dependence through the transnational system. The following conclusions are made: (1) Many of the charges against the Western news media and news services are without evidence. (2) The lack of differences among media of very different political systems argues against the theory of cultural imperialism. (3) Much of the rhetoric surrounding the New International Information Order debate addresses outdated questions. Stevenson concluded that this study helps clear up many of the questions in the pseudo debate.

31.

Riffe, Daniel. Spring 1984. "International News Borrowing: A Trend Analysis." *Journalism Quarterly*, 61(1):142–48.

This study assesses the extent of news borrowing from 1969–1979 by examining two constructed weeks per year of *The New York Times* and *Chicago Tribune*. It was found that roughly one of five foreign items in both papers contained second-hand information. The *Tribune* showed a growing trend in the use of borrowed news, despite overall reduced coverage. While correspondent news borrowing contributed very little to the overall borrowing trend, publication of wire service borrowed news grew significantly during the period studied. Results overall failed to establish a relationship between staffing and incidence of borrowed news published. Both papers showed distinct and significant patterns of greater publication of second-hand news from the Third World. Neither paper indicated any trend toward increased publication of second-hand news from the Second World. The *Times* showed a trend toward increased publication of second-hand news from Western (First World) nations.

32.

Aggarwala, Narinder K. 1983. "NIICO: Setting the Record Straight." *Media Asia*, 10(1):3–10.

Aggarwala argued that most of the issues and tenets surrounding the "free versus balanced information flow" debate did not originate with Third World governments or with UNESCO, but were raised in the 1950s by media and professional organizations of industrialized countries, particularly those of the United States, and that most people overlook that the New International Information and Communication Order (NIICO) deals with the totality of information, not just news media. He concluded that the challenge of NIICO is how to improve, strengthen, and expand information institutions and structures in the Third World so that the people there become beneficiaries and not victims of the "information revolution." To do this, Third World countries will need assistance to acquire and strengthen basic information capabilities.

33.

Cline, Carolyn G. Winter 1983. "The Myth of the Monolith." *Newspaper Research Journal*, 2:17–28.

To examine their coverage of world affairs, the author constructed a sample month of 28 issues at random for 1977 from 7 U.S. newspers (*Chicago Tribune*, *The Christian Science Monitor*, *Los Angeles Times*, *The Miami Herald*, *The New York Times*, *The Washington Post* and *The Wall Street Journal*). Stories were coded as to geographical area of origin, and Latin America stories were further coded as to country of origin and topic. A wide variance in Latin American coverage appeared in the papers, with a great range of news and topics. Only *The Miami Herald* offered a truly broad look at the continent; other papers followed their own patterns of news selection. *Chicago Tribune* saw Latin America as a setting for accidents and disasters; *Los Angeles Times* looked at it as a violent continent; *The Wall Street Journal* looked at the area's economic perspective; *The New York Times* covered official news; *The Washington Post* was undecided about the relative importance of war and violence on foreign relations. Thus, how the continent appeared to the reader depended on where the reader lived and which paper was read.

34.

Haque, Mazharul S. M. Fall 1983. "Is U.S. Coverage of News in Third World Imbalanced?" *Journalism Quarterly*, 60(3):521–24.

The author examined the allegation of quantitative imbalance in global coverage by *The New York Times*, *The Washington Post*, and *The Christian Science Monitor*. It was found that the *Times* devoted 13% of its total newshole to international news, while the *Post* devoted 10%, and the *Monitor* 21%. The space devoted to the Third World in the three dailies averaged 65% of the international news space. (69%, 64% and 62% for the *Post*, *Times* and *Monitor* respectively.) As for world attention by regional categories, the Near and Middle East topped with 30% of the foreign news space; Asia was second with 22%, and Western Europe accounted for only 16%. The newspapers depended heavily on their own correspondents. According to Haque, this finding reinforces the assumption that the number and distribution of correspondents is an important factor in the overall coverage of international news. As for front-page coverage, the Third World accounted for 82% of the foreign stories. Haque concluded that this study failed to show Western Europe as the centre of coverage.

35.

Nwosu, Ikechukwu E. 1983. "The Role of Research in the Global Information Flow Controversy: A Critical Analysis." *Gazette*, 31(2):79–88.

The global information flow controversy is perhaps the most topical and persistent issue in international communication and by extension, international politics today. One area of the controversy that seems not to have received adequate attention is the area of reliable research. The author critically reviewed some of the seminal studies of the world information flow problem as a means of demonstrating the need for more studies. One distinct feature found is the conflicting nature of the findings on the issues. There is a clearly drawn line of conflict between studies done by researchers sympathetic to the Western point of view in the debate and those done by researchers sympathetic to the Third World perspectives. It was concluded that an important step in resolving this conflict would be to subject already existing quantitative studies on this subject to serious replication exercises to test their validity and reliability.

36.

Payne, Les. October 1983. "The Problems of Third World Bias." *The ASNE Bulletin*, pp. 12–14.

Payne, the first American correspondent to visit guerrilla areas in what is now Zimbabwe in 1978 and 1979, talked about some of the Western biases in covering the Third World. Institutional bias, for instance, sending only white reporters to cover Africa, makes foreign correspondents particularly susceptible to manipulation by racist regimes. Individual bias results from political and cultural differences. In addition, foreign correspondents usually choose not to develop Third World sources, relying instead on handy, less reliable sources that reinforce stereotypes and misinform readers back home who have no way of double-checking news accounts.

37.

Shipman, John M. Winter 1983. "*New York Times*' Coverage of the War in El Salvador." *Journalism Quarterly*, 60(4):719–22.

On 10 February 1982, an editorial in *The Wall Street Journal* criticized *The New York Times*' coverage of the war in El Salvador. This study employed Hayakawa's trichotomy of sentence types—report sentences, inference sentences, and judgement sentences—to content analyse that coverage 25 days prior to the *Journal*'s attack and for 25 days after the attack. Results indicated that although the *Times'* editors were aware of the criticism, their style of writing did not change in response to that criticism. The number of attributed report sentences in the coverage (a measure of objectivity or the attempt to demonstrate objectivity) did not increase following the criticism. Most of the news stories came from government sources as routine news events or from rebel leaders. Shipman maintained that the low number of judgement sentences seemed to indicate that the *Times'* writers and editors exercised care not to put opinion in the form of judgements into news stories.

38.

Simon, Rita J. Fall 1983. "The Print Media's Coverage of the War in Lebanon." *Middle East Review*, 16(1):5–16.

Simon examined the coverage of 22 selected events in each war in Lebanon (the 1975/76 civil war and the 1982 war) in each of six major U.S. dailies. The views of the 1982 war expressed in eight major news and opinion magazines of the left, centre, and right from June to September 1982 were also examined. It was found that the six papers paid much more attention to the 1982 Israel–Lebanon war than they did to the Lebanese Civil War, a war in which more lives were lost and the destruction and chaos equally great. The ratio of front page stories about the Israel–Lebanon war as opposed to the Civil War was higher in *Chicago Tribune* and *The Christian Science Monitor* than in the other four papers. *The New York Times* was most balanced in the amount of headlines and front page coverage it gave to both wars. *The Wall Street Journal* was most consistently pro-Israel. Among the magazines, the three major weeklies, *Time*, *Newsweek*, and *U.S. News & World Report* were anti-Israel from the outset.

39.

Vilanilam, J. V. 1983. "Foreign Policy as a Dominant Factor in Foreign News Selection and Presentation: Case Study of Two Geographically and Culturally Distant Press Systems of the World." *Gazette*, 32(2):73–85.

Eight prominent newspapers from India and the U.S. were selected for this study. Of the 61 issues for each paper published during May and June, issues of 18 May, 2 June and 9 June were randomly selected, for a total of 24 issues. All foreign news in the three sample issues of each of the eight papers was examined. Results showed the two press systems differed significantly not only in the quantity of foreign news presented but also in the number of items. The U.S. papers carried a total of 491 items, whereas the Indian press system carried 514 items. However, the average area for an item in the U.S. papers was 24 column cm., as against 14 in the Indian system. The Indian papers gave more prominence to foreign news by placing more of it on the front page. The bulk of foreign news in the U.S. papers was supplied by the papers' own correspondents, whereas that in the Indian press system was supplied by AP, Reuters, and AFP, supporting the general perception of an imbalance in the flow of news.

40.

Abel, Elie. 1982. "Global Information: The New Battleground." *Political Communication and Persuasion*, 1(4):347–57.

The central paradox in the debate over the New World Information Order (NWIO) is that new communication technologies refused to be contained within national boundaries. The problem is accentuated by the fact that the technological power is concentrated in the hands of a relatively small number of industrialized countries. Consequently, less developed countries naturally favour measures of control over the information that flows in and out of their countries. A related problem is that the so-called NWIO has never been defined by any international body, not even by UNESCO.

41.

Gale, J. May 1982. "Reporting South Africa in Australia's Press." *Media Information Australia*, 24:27–33.

This study examined press reports related to South Africa that appeared in newspapers from the United Kingdom and Australia from 20 May to 10 June 1981. It was found that Australian papers varied considerably in the quantity of their news reports, but all relied heavily on news agency material and placed an undue emphasis on sports and violent events. Even *The Age* (considered the best of the three Australian papers surveyed) fell well behind the depth and range of news carried in the British quality press. Two major stories, both unfavourable to the image of South Africa, were not reported in any of the papers. *The Times* (London) provided detailed coverage of events in South Africa during the period studied. Its average story length for a given day was equal to that in *The Age* and *Advertiser*. Its coverage of South Africa on the whole contained a blend of specific detail, background and interpretation. Results indicated the need for more extensive, more thorough coverage of Africa by the Australian press.

42.

Hopple, Gerald W. Winter 1982. "International News Coverage in Two Elite Newspapers." *Journal of Communication*, 32(1):61–74.

This comparative study focused on *The New York Times* and *The Guardian* (Manchester)* in the first half of 1979. The author used data extracted from the papers as part of the World Event/Interaction Survey (WEIS)—an event data coding system that characterizes event/interaction or events in terms of an actor–initiator (who), target–recipient (whom), subject (what), and time (when). The WEIS scheme provides a set of clearly defined categories of activity which refer to the what component of an event. It was found that both papers contain a significant amount of non-overlapping material: overall, the *Times* reported more events for certain actors and the *Guardian* more events for others. The *Times* concentrated its coverage on the "superpowers," whereas the *Guardian* covered Western Europe, Asia, and Africa both regionally and in terms of specific countries. However, there was greater convergence when the focus was on salient activity or international "hot spots."

* *The Guardian* (Manchester) (1821) dropped its "Manchester" title in 1860 and two years later began to publish as a national newspaper.

43.

Lent, John A. April 1982. "ASEAN Mass Communication and Cultural Submission." *Media and Society*, 4(2):171–89.

Lent attempted to examine mass communication and cultural submission in the region of the Association of Southeast Asian Nations (ASEAN). Besides examining the complaint of these countries that they have been unduly influenced by outside media, an attempt is made in most instances to minimize those influences, and in at least one case, probably to reverse the procedure. The author concluded that ASEAN countries generally have been hospitable to outside media because of two factors: (1) As mass media (especially TV) are expensive endeavours, ruling elites find they must rely to a certain extent on outside media entrepreneurs. (2) There are hidden agenda that ruling elites hope for in setting media policy—keeping out negative Western values has more to do with keeping the national leadership stable than anything else.

44.

Masha, F. Lwanyantika. 1982. "Decolonizing Information: Toward a New World Information and Communication Order (NWICO)." *Political Communication and Persuasion*, 1(4):337–42.

Masha argues that the NWICO must be seen in the context of political and economic decolonization; the NWICO and New International Ecomomic Order (NIEO) are integral elements of the decolonization process. He argues further that the free flow of information across or even within cultures is neither possible nor desirable. Even if there were equal power, resources, access, and expertise for all—and clearly there are not—the result would be a "chaotic, confused, overloaded system of message transmission." Consequently, to have any kind of order, there must be regulation. The current debate centres on who should regulate. Noting that government ownership of media is manifest in the BBC, the VOA, and the Radio Moscow, the author maintains that each country should be free to decide questions of ownership and regulation without outside interference.

45.

McCoy, Jennifer and Elizabeth Cholawsky. Spring 1982. "News Sources on Rhodesia: A Comparative Analysis." *Journalism Quarterly*, 59(1):97–103.

The authors present the results of three months (May to July 1978) of coverage by four newspapers of the situation in Rhodesia prior to the 1979 elections. Coverage was judged in terms of biases and completeness. It was found that the Foreign Broadcast Information Service (FBIS) series for Sub-Saharan Africa tended to emphasize violent incidents involving black citizens and had generally unbiased coverage with the largest amount of background information. *The Christian Science Monitor* provided comparatively incomplete coverage of Rhodesia, and coverage was inconsistent with that provided by the three other sources. *The New York Times* provided a relatively unbiased picture of the Rhodesian situation, although its coverage was less complete than that of either FBIS or *The Times* (London). *The New York Times* generally reported both sides of conflicting stories, but provided relatively little background information. *The Times* (London) appeared to be the least biased of the four sources; its reports were generally consistent with the other sources, and contained all the viewpoints of specific incidents.

46.

Riffe, Daniel and Eugene Shaw. 1982. "Conflict and Consonance of Third World in Two U.S. Papers." *Journalism Quarterly*, 59(4):617–26.

The purpose of this study is to use a longitudinal design to explore trends in uniformity of foreign coverage in *The New York Times* and *Chicago Tribune*. A sample of two constructed weeks per year, i.e. 140 issue dates (10 years × 14 days) was randomly selected and coded. For the most part, the data supported the criticisms about Western coverage of the Third World. Although the results did not show any quantitative slighting of Third World events, there was a marked difference in topic emphases between Third World and First World news treatment—there were more conflict or upheaval stories in the Third World coverage. Topic agreement was high for both papers, but during the 10-year period studied, the consonance between the *Times* and the *Tribune* was most evident for Third World news. Results indicated that the American press, throughout the 1970s, continued to foster images of Third World nations as political systems rife with conflict.

47.

Sreberny-Mohammadi, Annabelle. February 1982. "More Bad News than Good: International News Reporting." *Media Information Australia*, 23:87–90.

Under the auspices of the International Association for Mass Communication Research (IAMCR) a project was set up that involved a content analysis of internatinal news reporting by 13 national teams. This study includes both quantitative and qualitative analysis of international news presentation and covers both a chronological and a composite week in the Spring of 1979. The author reports and discusses three key findings: (1) Politics dominated the international news reporting both in terms of topics covered and the actors presented, in all media systems; the four hard news categories (international politics, domestic politics, military/defense, and economics) accounted for the bulk of all stories, especially in the media of the developing countries. (2) In all national systems, most attention was paid to events happening within and actors belonging to the immediate geographical region. (3) In almost all these national media systems, news is defined as the exceptional event, so that coups and catastrophies were considered newsworthy wherever they occurred.

48.

Stein, M. L. January 1982. "UNESCO Debate Muted in Nairobi." *Quill*, pp. 10–11.

The UNESCO debate over Third World news reporting produces a muted echo in Nairobi (Kenya), the base for about 100 foreign correspondents who cover East Africa or the whole continent. Western journalists there generally reject the Third World charges that their reports from developing areas consist mainly of natural disasters, political unrest, bizarre customs and street crime. However, some correspondents tend to agree that in-depth reporting in a foreign land requires the correspondent a kind of commitment, sympathy and receptivity to the land and people. Some believe foreign journalists have an obligation to present a correct image and to create better understanding between peoples. Nevertheless, some maintain that distortion is built into the system because the news stories are to serve the home readers.

49.

Aggarwala, Narinder K. 1981. "The Issues at Stake and a New Information Model." *Media Development*, 28(1):7–12.

Athough Aggarwala agrees with the general tenor of developing countries' criticism of the Western media, particularly as it relates to the coverage of the Third World, he disagrees with the solutions proposed by the developing countries (including the Non-Aligned News Agencies Pool [NANAP]) to redress the situation. Instead, he proposes a model of an agency through which developing countries could get news about each other, and the industrial world, from their own perspective. The Third World News Agency (TWNA) would be a loose conglomerate of several autonomous regional news agencies. The structure of TWNA would allow it to collect and discriminate world news with multiple Third World perspectives. Structural components of the TWNA would include an international office, regional TWNAs, country bureaus, and international bureaus.

50.

Bador, Y. 1981. "News Exchange—the ASEAN Experience." *Media Asia*, 8(4):203–207.

Regional news exchanges in the Third World normally fail to live up to their expectations because participating agencies, being government-owned and controlled, usually flounder on the notion of news. The Association of Southeast Asian Nations (ASEAN) news exchange scheme has succeeded because its participants realized that to sell "protocol" or government news to each other will simply not work in the long run. Their new consensus to adhere to strict professional standards of news collection and distribution may well provide an example to others who contemplate similar ventures. There is a strong emphasis on speed, accuracy, and credibility. Member agencies are aware of the need to balance their objectives with the needs of their subscribers. The developmental form of journalism is being promoted in view of the public service nature of its objectives. A 12-point editorial guideline drawn up jointly by the member agencies sets out the principles for the news exchange.

51.

De Repentigny, Michel. June–August 1981. "The Daily Newspaper: Mirror of Our Myths." *Canadian Journal of Communication*, 8(1): 24–31.

The author argues that although Quebec's daily newspapers do not grant news from the Third World much importance, it should not be taken for granted that trying to improve this situation would contribute significantly to the advent of a New World Information Order. The problem is lack of production and circulation of information in developing countries. The author reviews news pertaining to the Third World in Quebec daily newspapers, and concludes that the commercial aspects of the news market in Western countries bear heavily on the "social vocation" of newspapers. The intimate structural ties between these two orders of necessity are such that not much can be done to require newspapers to offer their readers instructive information continually on the development processes of the Third World. What is most needed in the Third World is infrastructures that can generate and disseminate information horizontally among their inhabitants and those of other developing countries.

52.

"The Declaration of Talloires." July 1981. *Presstime*, pp. 26–27.

"We support the universal human right to be fully informed...." This is the declaration adopted unanimously by journalists from 20 countries at the Voices of Freedom Conference sponsored by Tufts University. Grounded in the concept of free flow of information, the declaration upholds that everyone has the right to freedom of opinion and expression without interference and regardless of frontiers.

53.

Gauhar, Altaf. "A Third World View." October 1981. *World Press Review*, p. 45.

The author starts out by arguing press freedom is not the same as free information flow because free trade is not the same as free movement of goods. Press freedom, he says, is a concept (or an ideal), whereas, what Western news agencies mean by free flow of information is a commercial proposition. Agency information or news is a commodity provided at a price determined by a transnational cartel of four news agencies. Contending that commercial considerations, cultural environment, the tastes and needs of a national audience as well as the judgement of an editor all determine what news is, he maintains that Western news agencies are not engaged in the business of truth but in reporting "newsworthy" events that can be sold for a profit. Therefore, he argues foreign journalists cannot demand unrestricted access to all official and unofficial sources of information in other countries, which is in fact denied in their own countries. The author concludes that in light of the fact that developing countries often face a dual challenge— one from authoritarian regimes of their own, and the other from rapacious Northern commercial managers—their determination to preserve their creative freedom and cultural identity is not a threat to press freedom.

54.

Kariel, Herbert G. and Lynn A. Rosenvall. Summer 1981. "Analysing News Origin Profiles of Canadian Daily Newspapers." *Journalism Quarterly*, 58(2):254–59.

The authors randomly selected a sample of 31 days representing 310 publishing days from 21 Canadian daily newspapers originating from 18 centres.* Datelines of each of the stories were recorded. In average, the data shows that local news had 37% of the total items, international news 31%, national news 19% and provincial news 12%. Forty-nine percent of the international news came from the U.S., 31% from Europe. Only about 20% came from the Third World. Factors that might explain the variations in the news origin profiles include: (1) isolation from the political, financial, industrial and cultural heartland; (2) the amount of importance of news generated in different types of cities; (3) linguistic affinities with regard to the location of a newspaper, the paper's readership and the news sources; and (4) foreign cultural and trade ties.

* The Canadian newspapers are: *Times-Colonist* (Victoria), *The Vancouver Sun,
Calgary Herald, Edmonton Journal, Leader-Post* (Regina), *Winnipeg Free Press,
Toronto Star, The London Free Press, Hamilton Spectator, Windsor Star, Ottawa
Journal, Le Droit* (Ottawa), *La Presse* (Montreal), *Montreal Star, Le Soleil*
(Quebec), *Gleaner Daily* (Fredericton), *Telegraph-Journal* (St. John's), *Chronicle-
Herald* (Halifax), *Guardian* (Charlottetown), and *Telegram* (St. John's). In each
city, the newspaper with the largest circulation was chosen. The newspapers
represented the federal capital, all provincial capitals and population centres over
100,000 persons. Since the Kitchener-Waterloo Record was unobtainable in the
original or on microfilm, the newspaper and this centre were left out of the
analysis.

55.

Manekar, D. R. 1981. "A Background to Alternative News Services:
History and Development." *Media Development*, 28(1):3–6.

The late 1970s have witnessed much activity in the area of communication and information within and among Third World countries.
Many developing countries have set up their own national news
agencies and quite a few have joined to organize news exchange
systems such as the Inter Press Service (IPS),* which is dedicated to
Third World needs exclusively and serves as a link between the Third
and First Worlds. Meanwhile, a group of experts from the West and
Third World have been meeting in recent years to discuss and finalize a
joint project described as a multinational news agency, devoted to the
collection and dissemination of development news from the Third
World. The author says that the fact that the Western news agencies have
been permitted to operate as freely as before in developing countries in
the past years, side by side with the Non-Aligned News Agencies Pool
(NANAP), has proved that the West's fear and accusations were
misplaced and that there was no ulterior motive behind the non-aligned
countries' move.

* Inter Press Service is a Rome-based news agency established by South American
countries in 1964. It adopts its own news values and reporting styles, which are
different from those in traditional Western journalism. It claims to report the
realities in South America and other Third World countries. In the mid-1980s, it has
about 450 media subscribers, mainly in Europe, the Middle East and the Third
World.

56.

Mehan, Joseph A. Fall 1981. "UNESCO and the U.S.: Action and Reaction." *Journal of Communication*, 31(4):159–63.

> The forces culmulating the MacBride Report were set in motion mostly by the United States. The U.S. worked to get Article 1, Section 2 written into the UNESCO charter, which says that "the organization would co-operate in advancing mutual knowledge and understanding … through all means of mass communications.…" Following quickly on this man-date, the U.S. proposed a year later that UNESCO establish a worldwide communications system. A statement by the U.S. National Commission in 1963 clearly encouraged U.N. system involvement in communication issues. In the late 1960s, the relationship between the U.S. and UNESCO cooled considerably. It was then that the concepts of two-way circulation of news and the balanced circulation of news were introduced. The first use of the term "New International Information Order" was in 1976 at the meeting of non-aligned countries in Tunisia. The declaration on mass media developed in the 1978 UNESCO 20th General Conference, and the MacBride Report of 1980, have been two of the major accomplish-ments of the international communications debate.

57.

Nordenstreng, Kaarle and A. Alanen. 1981. "Journalistic Ethics and International Relations." *Communication*, 6(2):225–54.

> A content analysis of 50 codes of ethics that included practically all existing contemporary journalistic codes revealed that particular aspects of international communication are largely neglected. Three codes out of five fail completely to cover international questions. To the extent that any consideration is given in these codes at the international level, best represented is the overall mandate to promote peace and security. Stand-ards concerning war propaganda and the nature of information dissemi-nated (truthfulness, objectivity) are practically absent from the codes. The topic of "free flow of information" has not been defined in these codes as more important than standards of objectivity, truthfulness, and equality. It is also found that international law includes several useful formulations with regard to developing the ethical codes of journalists, but it does not set many direct standards. Most of the codes refer

indirectly to the obligations of journalists mainly in terms of moral obligation and responsibility to keep the content of communications within the terms of international law.

58.

Power, Sarah Goddar. Fall 1981. "The U.S. View of Belgrade." *Journal of Communication*, 31(4):142–49.

Power suggests that the U.S. had three general, interrelated objectives with respect to information and communication issues at Belgrade: (1) to continue the trend with UNESCO toward more pragmatic and less controversial approaches to communications; (2) to blur North–South divisions on these issues and consolidate a working relationship with Third World moderates; (3) to isolate the Soviet and Third World radicals who have insisted on a restrictive approach to the press. The U.S. specifically sought to ensure non-controversial treatment of the Mac-Bride Report, and the establishment of the International Programme for Development of Communication (IPDC), a new UNESCO-based clearing house of information and communications development assistance.

59.

Qureshi, F. 1981. "Asian News Agencies—Strategy for Link-up." *Media Asia*, 8(3):75–81.

The author identifies some parameters within which an Asian news agency might work to promote South–South news. It is suggested that the Asian news link-up take the form of an Asian news pool, like the Non-Aligned News Agencies Pool. The character of the Asian news link-up must emphasize strongly the commitment to freedom of speech and free flow of information. The headquarter of the agency should be in a capital city of a country with the least restrictions, one which is not only democratic but also regarded as neutral in terms of Asian politics. The top policy-making body would be a board of directors composed of representatives of member nations. Management of the agency should be in the hands of professional editors and journalists selected from various Asian member countries.

60.

Raskin, A. H. Fall 1981. "U.S. News Coverage of the Belgrade UNESCO Conference." *Journal of Communication*, 31(4):164–74.

> Raskin examined 448 news clippings and 206 editorials from newspapers in all parts of the U.S.* and found not even one story which dealt with UNESCO's basic activities but 173 news and feature stories dealing with the debate over communications policy. The debate was also the central topic of 181 editorials. Without exception the editorials expressed apprehension about UNESCO's attempts to help establish policy in matters affecting the "free flow of information." The news events that got the widest press coverage and the greatest prominence were those that reinforced the fears expressed on the editorial pages. Overall, coverage focused almost exclusively on Western worries about the UNESCO initiative, with little presentation of opposing viewpoints. The majority (80%) of the stories were from AP and UPI. The author concluded that the distortion of news stories on Belgrade was not created in editorialization but in the process of news selection.

> * The author directly checked the files of *The New York Times*, *The Washington Post*, *The Wall Street Journal* and *Los Angeles Times*. The remaining clips were obtained through monitoring large and small newspapers by Press Intelligence, Inc.

61.

Ravault, Rene-Jean. Fall 1981. "Information Flow: Which Way Is the Wrong Way?" *Journal of Communication*, 31(4):129–34.

> The author argues that the MacBride Report's* recommendations would help stop the rapidly detoriorating military, diplomatic and economic situation of the Anglo-American countries from which the most important international communication flow originates. The recommendations seeking to put an end to the cultural and communication domination of the developed countries are based on a sender-oriented conception of the communication process which sees receivers (recipients of products of mass culture) as passive. Thus the Report suggests that "passive receivers" (developing countries) can escape this detrimental situation by becoming news "senders" with access to the institutions of expression

and diffusion or broadcasting of their own culture. The crucial role of the receivers' experience and language in the recreation of the meaning of imported technical, scientific and strategic data is acknowledged but not acted upon by the Report.

* UNESCO formed a commission headed by Sean MacBride, an Irish journalist and lawyer, to study international communication problems in 1977. After three years' effort, the MacBride Report was finally completed and published in the title *Many Voices, One World* (see Entry No. 152). It maintains that there is not a universal model of communication system that suits all countries in the world due to historical, economic, cultural and social differences among them. In addition, it calls for reducing the imbalance and deficiencies in international information flow, supporting countries to adopt communication policies that suit their own realities. Some of the recommendations of the Report for the improvement of international news coverage include: (1) to establish self-policing journalists' organizations to encourage responsibility, (2) to devise an international code of ethics for journalists, (3) to publish more foreign news with background and analysis, particularly news from the developing countries, and (4) to set up press councils and ombudsmen to whom people who have grievances against the news media may appeal.

62.

Righter, Rosemary. October 1981. "The Global News Battle." *World Press Review*, pp. 41–42.

Third World critics charge Western media for ill reporting their countries. On the other hand, Western news agencies argue that they provide more news (including development news) than Third World or Western newspapers can use and that they cannot force their news subscribers to use what they do not like to print. Righter points out the 1976 Summit of Non-Aligned Countries in Colombo formally endorsed the call for a New World Information Order (NWIO) as "an integral part of the overall struggle for political, economic and social independence." Then after the UNESCO General Conference in Nairobi, a commission was set up to survey communications problems and seek ways to establish a new order, which resulted in the publication of the MacBride Report in 1980—a compromise between the two sides.

63.

Rimmer, Tony. 1981. "Foreign News on UPI's Wire in the U.S.A." *Gazette*, 28(1):35–49.

The author content analysed the UPI wire stories for six days, 13–18 February 1977. A 15-category class for news-gathering source was used to see whether there were differences between the news sources across different regions. There was a total of 604 stories: 214 of which were about foreign (non-U.S.) news topics. Of the stories, 141 (65%) were about politics and 31 (14%) were about crime, disaster and public safety. Economic activity, science, and cultural matters made up 11% of the foreign stories. Foreign stories originating in the U.S. dominated with 50 (23%) items, followed by Britain, the U.S.S.R., Uganda and Israel. It was concluded that the flow of news was largely pro-Western and that the coverage of Third World events and issues was superficial, focusing largely on violence and disasters rather than positive developments. The study also provided a detailed analysis of UPI's Latin American coverage for the week.

64.

Roach, Colleen. Fall 1981. "French Press Coverage of the Belgrade UNESCO Conference." *Journal of Communication*, 31(4):175–87.

The author analysed 97 articles from Parisian and regional dailies, weekly and monthly magazines,* and 99 AFP dispatches for the period 19 September to 5 November 1980. The communications debate was the subject of or was mentioned in 51 of the articles and 48 of the dispatches. Most of the other articles dealt with "spot-news" items unrelated to any of the substantive questions discussed at Belgrade. The French press almost invariably presented UNESCO's communications activities as the most important and controversial subject. The major items on the communications agenda were identified as the MacBride Report and the International Programme for Development of Communication (IPDC). None of the articles or criticism that claimed the MacBride Report justified government control of the media were backed up by excerpts from the Report itself. Overall, French press coverage of Belgrade included very few news items on Third World positions or statements, gave priority to Western opinions, and highlighted the positions of the Soviet bloc.

* The French newspapers in this study are *Liberation* and *Le Monde*, and the French magazines are *Quotidien de Paris* and *Jeune Afrique* published in Africa.

65.

Sadar, Zianddin. February 1981. "Between GIN and TWIN: Meeting the Information Needs of the Third World." *Aslib Proceedings*, 33(2):53–61.

As a result of the United Nations Conference of Science and Technology for Development, Third World countries were to establish a Global Information Network (GIN) that will give open access to developing countries to scientific and technological information from the industrialized nations. However, in the absence of financial support, GIN will probably remain a paper agreement. Sadar suggests that developing countries develop a Third World Information Network (TWIN) to share locally produced science and technology information as another alternative.

66.

Singh, Kussun and Bertran Gross. Fall 1981. "'MacBride': The Report and Response." *Journal of Communication*, 31(4):104–17.

Reviewing the MacBride Report and its related matters, the authors suggest that the most innovative part of this report is the sections on the democratization of communication. Members in the Commission recommend horizontal communication, counter-communication and three forms of alternative information as a means of resisting un-democratic political systems. Scholars who had contributed to the IAMCR reader edited by Cees Hamelink criticized the MacBride Report for being unable to meet Third World demands and for the failure to address the specific question of transnational transfer of technologies. But members from Western news organizations argue that recommendations in the Report would seriously interfere with press freedom and the free flow of information.

67.

Torchia, Andrew. May/June 1981. "Assignment: Africa." *Columbia Journalism Review*, p. 41

Torchia, a foreign correspondent covering East Africa for the Associated Press, talks about some of the problems in covering Africa. Besides inadequacies of language, cultural background and organizational constraints, he pointed out that a foreign rather than an African perspective and lack of commitment to the African continent are also important factors affecting the qualities of the coverage of Africa.

68.

"Confrontations at Talloires." 1 June 1981. *Time*, p. 82.

Western representatives from 60 news organizations of 24 countries including AP, UPI, Reuters and AFP, conferred at Talloires (France) in common opposition to the UNESCO's proposals to regulate the world's press through the debate of the New World Information Order. The meeting, sponsored by the World Press Freedom Committee, was a direct response to UNESCO's Belgrade conference in October 1980 in which the MacBride Report was adopted.

69.

Weaver, David H. and G. Cleveland Wilhoit. Spring 1981. "Foreign News Coverage in Two U.S. Wire Services." *Journal of Communication*, 31(2):55–63.

The authors content analysed wire service copy from the AP and UPI services flowing into the computer of the *Indiana Daily Student* to examine the quantity and quality of news about foreign lands available to most small-to-medium sized mass media in the United States. Two types of samples—two weeks of consecutive days, and two "constructed weeks" both in 1979—were used. It was found that the most frequently covered less developed countries in the "official" wire service sample were Iran, Uganda, Israel, Egypt, China, and Nicaragua. Contrary to expectations, there were more foreign news stories from the less developed countries in both the AP and UPI regional wires, and these stories were, on the average, longer than those from the more developed countries. Stories from the less developed countries were significantly more likely than stories from the more developed countries to be about diplomatic or political activity between states, internal conflict or crisis, armed conflict, and political crime.

70.

Womack, Brantly. Summer 1981. "Attention Maps of 10 Major Newspapers." *Journalism Quarterly*, 58(2):260–65.

Womack reported the results of the Attention Map project, which involved measuring the amount of general news devoted to geographical areas for the week of 23–29 July 1979, in 10 major U.S. and European newspapers.* The geographical categories of analysis were local city, local state, nations, international regions and world. Each category of raw data on news attention patterns was converted into percentage of coverage per newspaper-day, and all comparisons were in terms of percentages. The general result was that while all newspapers had a local point of view in their news coverage, attention mapping displays significant differences in the components and the scale of localization. Further analysis of international coverage showed that localization affects international content and the selective attention of various papers supplied quite different world views to their readership.

* The 10 major newspapers are: *The New York Times*, *The Washington Post*, *The Miami Herald*, *The Boston Globe*, *Fort Worth Star-Telegram*, *Houston Chronicle*, *Daily Telegraph* (London), *Le Soir* (Belgium), *France-Soir* and *Frankfurter Allgemeine Zeitung* (Federal Republic of Germany).

71.

Zassoursky, Yassen and Sergei Losev. Fall 1981. "Information in the Service of Progress." *Journal of Communication*, 31(4):118–21.

The authors contend that the MacBride Report represents a serious contribution to the cause of placing information in the service of peace and progress by encouraging the formation of a new information procedure based on respect for national sovereignty in the field of information and culture. They agree with the Report that it is very important to rid imperialist dominance in the spiritual life of developing countries. The

Report criticized the commercial approach of Western countries to information activities. It mentions the need to "reduce the negative influence of the market and of commercial considerations on the content and organization of national and international information flows."

72.

Brown, Trevor. Spring 1980. "Did Anybody Know His Name? U.S. Press Coverage of Biko." *Journalism Quarterly*, 57(1):31–38.

Brown examined the indexes of *The New York Times* and *The Washington Post* from 1969 to 1977. He found that between the founding of the South African Students' Organization (SASO) in 1969 and Steven Biko's death in 1977, in its almost annual series between 1969 and 1977 on South Africa in general, the *Times* focused on others than Biko. Therefore, the paper's assertions about Biko's stature and significance after his death were startling. Results were similar in the *Post*. The author concluded that this study confirms the observations on newspapers' lack of perspective or interpretation, on correspondents' dealing with political discontinuities, and on the anchorage of press coverage in the immediate present.

73.

Chalkley, A. 1980. "Development Journalism—A New Dimension in the Information Process." *Media Asia*, 7(4):215–17.

Chalkley suggests ways to make development journalism more readable, interesting, colourful, and informative: (1) Simplify technical jargons into language as close as possible to everyday speech. (2) Humanize the economic and social story, using colourful phrases and keeping the copy lively, without a loss of accuracy. (3) Illustrate stories with pictures, charts or diagrams. (4) The subject matter must change to relate stories to the lives of the ordinary people. (5) Cover broader national and international trends.

74.

Cuthbert, Marlene. 1980. "Reaction to International News Agencies: 1930s and 1970s Compared." *Gazette*, 26(4):99–110.

Cuthbert pointed out the phenomenon of international news agencies' hegemony during both the 1930s and the 1970s. In the 1930s, it was the European agencies' hegemony amidst voices of objection to the partitioning of the world according to the interests of a few who had the means to communicate. Many who didn't could only call for a free flow of information, which meant largely freedom from *de jure* control over the agencies' domination of information. In the 1970s, the Third World believed that freedom of information could exist only when all parties concerned had equal access to the channels. Hence, they emphasized a balanced flow and freedom from the *de facto* control of world information by the most powerful.

75.

Cuthbert, Marlene. August 1980. "Canadian Newspaper Treatment of a Developing Country: The Case of Jamaica." *Canadian Journal of Communication*, 7(1):16–31.

Cuthbert analysed all Jamaican coverage in three Canadian dailies (*Montreal Star*, *Ottawa Citizen*, and *Toronto Star*) for 1976 and January 1977. All coverage of Jamaica except advertisements was coded as to placement, dateline, column inches, source, headline, headline subject, article subject, and article treatment (positive or negative). Overall, Jamaica was portrayed as a politically divided, unstable, crime-ridden society. Much more hard news of crime and violence than soft news was found. There were few developmental stories, but they tended to be longer with more interpretation. Reuter was the major source of news on Jamaica providing more than one-third of the stories in the three papers: AP provided only 10.8% and Canada's own news service, Canadian Press (CP)* provided only 5%. Analyses of trends and developments over time were largely ignored. Cuthbert concluded that in this case press coverage of the Third World is biased and inadequate.

* The Canadian Press is a national news co-operation founded in Toronto in 1917. It has 104 daily newspaper members.

76.

Kliesch, Ralph E. Summer 1980. "News Media Presence and Southeast Asia." *Journalism Quarterly*, 57(2):255–61.

This study was based on field research undertaken in the summer of 1978 in Thailand, Malaysia, Singapore and Indonesia. Its purpose was to ascertain the relationship between the presence of foreign news media and the countries' own journalistic outlook on the rest of the world. Interviews were conducted with senior correspondents of international media, information officers of both national governments and foreign embassies, and with all resident correspondents. Kliesch found that only a relative handful of the world's nations (Japan, U.S., Britain, Hong Kong, France, Australia, West Germany) are directly involved in the international collection of news. Vast regions of Southeast Asia and the Third World in general, had little or no direct news-seeking contact with one another. The most heavily covered region was Thailand, yet it had the smallest number of full-time correspondents abroad. Singapore, a major base for foreign newsmen, had a large staff of correspondents abroad. The media focus on the four nations studied tended to fall reciprocally on those nations that cover the region most heavily.

77.

Nwosu, Ikechukwu E. 1980. "Towards a New World Information Order: Recommendations Based on a Comparative Study of Selected Western Prestige Newspapers' Coverage of Black Africa." *Media Asia*, 7(2):81–90.

Black Africa was underreported. Nwosu arrived at such a conclusion after examining the coverage of Black Africa from October 1977 to January 1978 in four British and American prestige newspapers.* Undue emphasis was laid on sensational African news and a de-emphasis of news and opinion about African development, culture and arts. Nwosu proposed that a theoretical model, the New World Information Achievement Continuum be used as a framework for possible solutions to the problem of information flow. In the model, the present order, A, is given a negative sign "–" while the New Order, B, is given a positive sign "+" and is considered an ideal type. The distance between A and B is the operational continuum, a progression from A to B is considered a positive gain.

* The four Western prestige newspapers are: *The New York Times*, *The Christian Science Monitor*, *The Times* (London) and *The Guardian*.

78.

Perry, Marna. June 1980. "ANPA Tells UNESCO of MacBride Report Dangers." *Presstime*, p. 14.

The American Newspaper Publishers Association (ANPA) maintains that the MacBride Report, being biased against private enterprise, gears toward media control by the government. The Association's list of particularly worrisome recommendations of the Report includes effective legal measures to limit concentration and monopolization, circumscribing the action of transnations by requiring them to comply with "national legislation and developmental policies," and the shift of the focus of the right of reply and correction from what the reader wants to read to "what a government official believes the reader ought to read."

79.

Pratt, C. B. 1980. "The Reportage and Image of Africa in Six U.S. News and Opinion Magazines: A Comparative Study." *Gazette*, 26(1):31–45.

This article reviewed a 1976 image study on the depth of African coverage in six American news and opinion magazines (*Time*, *Newsweek*, *U.S. News & World Report*, *The Nation*, *New Republic* and *National Review*)* and the image they presented to their readers. The author found more similarities than differences in the treatment of Africa by the magazines. The major discrepency was found in the U.S. political stances of the opinion journals. In general, they call for a firm policy in Africa in order to check the pervasiveness of Communist gains. All of the magazines portrayed Africa as conflict-ridden. In terms of quantity, there was very little African news which presented Africa as an unstable, politically gullible continent whose course of action was dependent primarily on the U.S. and the Soviet Union. Less than one-fifth of the 58 nations in Africa were covered.

Time (1923) and *Newsweek* (1933) are prestige weekly news magazines in the U.S.A. The former has a circulation of 4,720,000 and the latter 3,181,000. *National Review* (1955) has a fortnightly circulation of 117,000. *The Nation* (1865), a weekly magazine tilting toward the left in politics, has a circulation of 85,000. *New Republic* (1914), tilting toward the right, has a circulation of 90,000.

80.

Said, Edward W. 1980. "U.S. Coverage of the Iran Crisis: An Assessment." *Media Asia*, 7(2):62–70.

Said contended that the American media (*The New York Times*, *St. Louis Post-dispatch*, *Chicago Tribune*, *The Wall Street Journal*, *Time*, *Newsweek*, and television networks) presented Iran as a militant, dangerous, and anti-American country. He claimed that these media did little to provide Americans with a balanced, thorough treatment of the social, political and economic events in Iran that led to the revolution, the Shah's exile, and the hostage crisis. In addition, these biases against Iran were disseminated throughout the world by American wire services.

81.

Said, Edward W. March–April 1980. "Iran." *Columbia Journalism Review*, pp. 23–33.

Said discussed how the American public, through the eyes of the media, evaluated Iran during and following the U.S. Embassy seige, suggesting that the U.S. media created a negative image of Iran on the basis of one isolated incident. Although the media provided a great deal of coverage, there was actually very little real information. Said said the news media regarded the Pahlavi regime with unmitigated disdain and suspicion. In the last part of the article, the U.S. media coverage of the seige was found to be imbalanced in comparison with the European coverage.

82.

Savio, Roberto. 1980. "Why the World Needs a New Information Order." *Media Asia*, 7(3):145–49.

Savio argues that the New World Information Order is more than anything else a qualitative problem. The problem for Third World countries is not so much to produce more news items as to produce news items different from those in the present flow of information that represent values, realities and priorities not present now. The crux of the issue is that the present information system was born out of the market, which has created its own rules, values, and priorities. Consequently, the news flow is event-oriented rather than process-oriented. This has led to the exclusion from the information process of social sectors which do not belong to the market. Therefore, it is necessary for both the Western and Third World countries to use new techniques, new ideas and new content to dismantle the present vertical information structure and create new horizontal structures.

83.

Stevenson, Robert L. and Mark T. Greene. Spring 1980. "A Reconsideration of Bias in the News." *Journalism Quarterly*, 57(1):115–21.

The authors raised three conceptual problems with the traditional approach to the study of news bias. They hypothesized that most people define bias in the news as information which is discrepant with the mental picture they already hold about the situation and applied Carter's signalled stopping technique to leave a trace of their cognitive behaviour. They concluded the hypothesis was supported and contended that news bias is less a function of reporters' accuracy or fairness and more a function of what readers and viewers think the situation is or ought to be.

84.

Tadayon, Mohamed. 1980. "The Image of Iran in *The New York Times*." *Gazette*, 26(4):217–33.

The author content analysed a total of 509 items of news reports, stories, commentaries and letters to the editors related to *The New York Times'* coverage of Iran in the period from 1971 to 1976. Results showed that in the period from 1973 to 1974, mention of the Shah and Iran's oil income steadily rose while mention of Iran's arms purchase from the United States declined. In the period from 1974 to 1976, mention of the Shah declined relative to stories on arms purchase from the U.S. and involvement of multinational companies with Iran and its great oil income.

Detection of U.S.–Shah tension assumed increasing importance in coverage. There was a conspicuous absence of mention of religious opposition to the Shah's regime, although that turned out to be a major force in the uprisings and eventual overthrow of the Shah. The effect of the 1973–1974 oil crisis, in which Organization of Petroleum Exporting Countries (OPEC) increased prices drastically, was to firmly introduce oil and oil riches as a major element in the image of Iran.

85.

"That's No Way to Say Goodbye." 28 January 1980. *Time*, p. 84.

American newsmen were deported from Iran and Afghanistan. In Iran, a government official said that they were out of touch with reality and unfair to Iran and its revolution. In Afghanistan, the chief press censor, Gul Ahmed Faried, a journalism graduate of Columbia University, said that American bourgeois journalists did not write for the benefit of the masses.

86.

Charles, Jeff, Larry Shore and Rusty Todd. Spring 1979. *"The New York Times* Coverage of Equatorial and Lower Africa." *Journal of Communication*, 29(2):148–55.

The authors examined *The New York Times'* coverage of Southern Africa based on half-year samples from *The New York Times Index* for the years 1960, 1965, 1970 and 1975. Angola, Kenya, South Africa, Rhodesia, and Zaire together accounted 77.4% of the coverage. South Africa led the coverage with 34.5%. In three of these countries, coverage was related to transitional turmoil such as civil disorders and revolutions. Violence was found to be much effective in getting into the front pages. In addition, trade, telecommunications, traffic and population were strongly related to news coverage.

87.

Dorman, William A. and Ehsan Omeed. Jan./Feb. 1979. "Reporting Iran the Shah's Way." *Columbia Journalism Review*, pp. 27–33.

The authors argue that the American news coverage of the Iranian Revolution is systematically biased against the opposition forces of the Shah that are portrayed as fanatical and irrational. The use of code words such as "mobs," "riots," "anarchy" and "rampage" all reflect this bias. The Shah's ruling methods are also covered critically, but his motives and goals go almost unquestioned. The U.S. news media, they say, ignored the real motives of the Iranian people: redressing gross economic inequality and ending 26 years of absolute political repression. In addition, the bias of Western journalists lies in differences of religion and culture. For instance, judged by Western standards, non-Christian clergy and religious practices are regarded as "other"—with little legitimacy. Also, Western journalists had little understanding of Iranian customs. Therefore, it is concluded that Americans are misinformed by biased pro-Shah coverage.

88.

Hartgen, Stephen. Summer 1979. "How Four Papers Covered the Communist Chinese Revolt." *Journalism Quarterly*, 56(2):175–78.

Hartgen examined the China coverage in *The Atlanta Constitution, Cleveland Plain Dealer, Louisville Courier-Journal* and *Minneapolis Tribune* in 1945 and 1946 in order to discover how these American regional newspapers explained China events in context. The author used a five-point scale to measure the interpretive content of China events. Two important events were chosen for analysis: (1) the resignation of U.S. Ambassador Patrick Hurley; and (2) the indecisive Manchurian battles between the Communists and the Nationalists. It was found that coverage of the first event contained more interpretation than coverage of the second. The author concluded that the papers lack sustained analysis of China news, which was just important enough for some commentary. Thus, it was not possible for the papers to provide their readers with information that might help set the China events in perspective.

89.

Kaplan, Frank. 1979. "The Plight of Foreign News in the U.S. Mass Media." *Gazette*, 25(4):233–43.

The author points out the insufficiency in the amount, scope and type of international news disseminated by U.S. mass media, particularly from the Third World countries of Africa, Asia and Latin America. International news agencies (AP, UPI, AFP, Reuters, and TASS) represent the news from a self-centred perspective influenced by the political ideology, value system and perceived national interests of their own countries. Although the technology for facilitating information flow has advanced, the coverage of foreign events is decreasing and the number of full-time correspondents abroad for American media is on the decline.

90.

Masmoudi, Mustapha. 1979. "A New World Information Order." *Journal of Communication*, 29(2):172–85.

Masmoudi, the former minister of information in Tunisia and member of the MacBride Commission, might well represent the Third World grievances and complaints. He indicated that the flow of information in the world was characterized by seven basic imbalances: (1) a flagrant quantitative imbalance between North and South; (2) an inequality in information resources; (3) a *de facto* hegemony and a will to dominate; (4) a lack of information on developing countries; (5) survival of the colonial era; (6) an alienating influence in the economic, social, cultural spheres; and (7) messages ill-suited to the area in which they are disseminated.

91.

Mishra, V. M. Summer 1979. "News from the Middle East in Five U.S. Media." *Journalism Quarterly*, 56(2):374–78.

Mishra content analysed the news from the Middle East in four U.S. "elite newspapers" and a television network to (1) delineate the flow of news from the Middle East in relation to the news from other regions of the world, (2) examine the pattern of news coverage from the region by the media, and (3) determine the direction (unfavourable, neutral, favourable or mixed) of the coverage. It was found that the coverage was mostly concentrated on Israel, Egypt, and Iran. The *Chicago Tribune* had the least space and *The Washington Post* the most space devoted to the items from the region. *The New York Times* provided more pictorial items and gave most attention to hard news. *Los Angeles Times* provided more interpretive news features and the *Post* offered more opinion columns. In addition, most items dealing with the internal and external politics, Arab–Israeli conflict, human interest and American interest were treated in a neutral and professional journalistic fashion. More economic, social and national development items were treated positively than negatively.

92.

Morris, Roger. March/April 1979. "Reporting the Race War in Rhodesia." *Columbia Journalism Review*, pp. 32–34.

Morris indicated that the U.S. newspaper coverage of Rhodesia, especially the war, was full of "racial overtones." The news on Whites tended to figure on the front page, while important events concerning the Blacks were dismissed as if insignificant. The latter were often presented in a distorted and shallow manner. Morris said the coverage resulted from racial segregation, editorial pressures from home offices, severe restrictions that were imposed on journalists by the Smith regime, and the reporters' inability or unwillingness to report the Black side of the conflict.

93.

Sreebny, Daniel. Spring 1979. "American Correspondents in the Middle East: Perceptions and Problems." *Journalism Quarterly*, 56(1):386–88.

Sreebny attempts to find out who the American correspondents in the Middle East were, how they perceived their jobs, and what problems they faced in covering the area in the 1970s. Findings include: (1) American correspondents there have an average of 20 years of news experience; on average, 14 of these years are served as foreign correspondents and five-and-a-half years in the Middle East. (2) They covered a wide range of geographic areas; fewer than 10% worked in only one country; 39% covered 15 or more countries. (3) Most are familiar with languages other than English, but few know the regions's major language. Problems include biased coverage by the U.S. media, censorship and restrictions, cultural gap and distrust of American reporters throughout the region. It is concluded that the knowledge of American correspondents is limited and U.S. coverage of the Middle East tends to emphasize what has happened, ignoring what may happen.

94.

Beikaoui, Janice Monti. Winter 1978. "Images of Arabs and Israelis in the Elite Press, 1966–74." *Journalism Quarterly*, 55(4):732–38.

To examine the shifting images of Arabs and Israelis, the author content analysed a sample of 442 articles from *Time, Newsweek, U.S. News and World Report* and the *Sunday New York Times* around the Arab–Israeli wars in June 1967 and October 1973. Two indicators of image were used. Verbs and adverbs synonymous with "said," "tell" and "ask" were coded in the Attributional Image category that represents the publications' method of attributing a style or an image to a speaker's manner of address. Judgemental adjectives and descriptive phrases were coded in the Descriptive Image category that represents the publications' most direct editorial means of image creation. The author coded both categories for direction on a three-point scale: favourable, neutral and unfavourable. Descriptive image content was also classified into thematic and role categories for both Israeli and Arab referents. Two hypotheses were supported: (1) The prestige press reflected a more favourable image of Arab actors in the period around October 1973 than June 1967. (2) The mass-appeal press is slower than the prestige press to reflect image change was supported.

95.

Beltran, Luis Ramiro. 1978. "Communication and Cultural Domination: USA–Latin American Case." *Media Asia*, 5(4):183–92.

Beltran argues that Latin America is dominated by U.S. cultural imperialism; there is no two-way flow between the U.S. and Latin America. Both in terms of quantity and quality, U.S. communication input to Latin America is enormous and influential. By omission and commission, U.S. reporting on Latin American countries is systematically superficial and consistently biased. Furthermore, this bias in favour of U.S. and Western

Europe news and against Latin American cultural and political news has been transplanted to the Latin American journalism profession.

96.

Hester, Al. September 1978. "Newsworthiness: Toward a New Concept." *Democratic Journalist*, pp. 16–18.

Western news agencies, recognizing discontent from Third World clients, should consider emphasizing news that builds and supports societal growth instead of the old newsworthiness standards of stress and violence.

97.

Merrill, John C. Winter/Spring 1978. "The 'Free Flow' of News among News." *Nieman Report*, pp. 44–46.

Merrill defends the practice of Western journalism which is harshly attacked by Third World critics. The fundamental issue is that Western media distort realities and present basically negative images of the developing countries. Pointing out basic conceptual differences between the Third and Western Worlds, he lays out what the Third World wants— balanced flow, unbiased coverage, and more development news. He argues that unevenness of flow and "biased" in the sense of being unfaithful to reality and manipulated by journalistic judgement are basic characteristics of news in any context; the atypical, unusual, and often sensational nature of news is a very basic part of the definition of news in the Western world. He concludes that Third World editors are doing the same things which they criticize are done by Western news media.

98.

Righter, Rosemary. Summer 1978. "Is Western-Style Journalism Appropriate to the Third World?" *Nieman Report*, pp. 30–32.

Righter explains why many Third World countries perceive Western-style journalism as inappropriate to their own countries. Developing countries have different understanding of the Western notion of freedom of expression or of the press. Third World spokesmen argue that they do not seek to block the free flow of information, but to make it genuinely free—free of the domination exercised by the powerful few, free of "alien" values, free "to defend the interests of the society as a whole, and the rights of the entire people." As the present international media system is serving primarily the Western industrial complex that perpetuates the global status quo by exposing developing countries to "inappropriate patterns of consumption, values and life-styles," developing countries must regard the "decolonization" of information as priority over other considerations. Finally, she suggests that journalists coordinate with governments on an international basis and demonstrate to them the value of free flow of information. To achieve this task, they need to take the stigma of "Westernism" out of Western-style journalism.

99.

Lent, John A. Winter 1977. "Foreign News in American Media." *Journal of Communication*, 27(1):46–51.

This study outlines four general factors affecting the quality and use of foreign news in the U.S. media: (1) international diplomacy, national government and military policies, and historical-cultural heritage consideration; (2) crisis-oriented coverage and usage; (3) censorship policies and image building activities of other countries; (4) shrinking corps of adequately trained correspondents abroad. The U.S. is primarily seen as a major news source rather than a receiver because of its status as a big power and of its pervasive, worldwide network of news agencies.

100.

Semmel, Andrew K. 1977. "The Elite Press, the Global System and Foreign News Attention." *International Interactions*, 3(4):317–28.

Semmel examined proximity in the flow of news in *The New York Times*, *The Miami Herald*, *Los Angeles Times* and *Chicago Tribune*. It was found that news is heavily concentrated on a small number and percentage of countries, with the focus of attention on the rich, the politically potent and culturally Western societies. The foreign news in the elite press is found to be Western-oriented, dominated by big powers, and

Euro-centric. The author also indicated that the majority of countries are unable to overcome the traditional indifference of the press. He developed a "perceptual distance" measurement between national actors based on the economic, political and cultural positions a country occupies in the global system relative to the U.S. The economic variable was chosen as the most representative category. There are also some other findings pertinent to the nature of foreign news, which has implications for Western press coverage of the Third World.

101.

Waters, Harry F. September 1976. "A Bow to Big Brother?" *Newsweek*, pp. 69–70.

Representatives of 85 nations endorse the idea of creating a joint Third World news agency that would supplant the Western wire services operating in their countries. And a UNESCO-sponsored conference in Costa Rica of 21 Latin American countries attacks Western news agencies and proposes three resolutions which "lifted the eyebrows of free press advocates."

Part II

Books, Book Chapters, Monographs, Papers and Reports

102.

Kelly, James D. 2–5 July 1988. "El Salvador and Nicaragua in Four Elite U.S. Newspapers: Multiple Images and the Journalist's Reporting Perspective." Paper presented at the 71st Annual Meeting of the Association for Education in Journalism and Mass Communication held in Portland, Oregon.

> The author examined the images of the governments of El Salvador and Nicaragua in four elite U.S. newspapers during 1983, with a primary focus on the frequency and direction of mention. The purpose was to discern whether an overall image of a foreign country is a reasonable manifestation of how that country is presented in mass media, or whether such an overall measure is too broad. Results indicated considerable differences between the images presented by domestic and foreign reporters, probably due to the differences in the informational sources they consult and quote in their reports rather than any overt bias. In addition, findings suggest that there is a relationship between the policy position of the U.S. government toward the governments of El Salvador and Nicaragua and the types of coverage those two governments receive in the elite press of the U.S.

103.

Slawen, Machael B. and Lee Jung-sook. 3–5 March 1988. "Terrorism and the Crash of KAL Flight 858: A Comparison of U.S. and South Korean Newspaper Coverage." Paper presented at the Spring Conference of the Mass Communication Division of the Association for Education in Journalism and Mass Communication held in Boston, Massachusetts.

> The authors compared U.S. and South Korean press coverage of the crash of the Korean Air Lines Flight 858 on 29 November 1987 to examine how the press reported the terrorist angle before evidence supporting the charges of terrorism was uncovered. Stories dealing with the crash from 30 November to 3 December 1987 were analysed. The data shows no evidence that the press sensationalizes terrorist events. Other findings include: (1) Neither the South Korean nor the U.S. press gave much coverage to the terrorist angle until a major event was

uncovered suggesting North Korean involvement. (2) Mere allegations or rumors of terrorism alone will not lead the press to report about terrorism in great detail.

104.

Culbertson, Hugh M. 1–4 August 1987. "Agenda Diversity: A Comparison of American and Filipino Editorials on the 1986 Election and Revolution." Paper presented at the Annual Meeting of the Association for Education in Journalism and Mass Communication held in San Antonio, Texas.

> The author compared the differences of editorials about the 1986 election and revolution in the Philippines in four prestigious newspapers (*The Christian Science Monitor*, *The Wall Street Journal*, *The New York Times* and *The Washington Post*) and two Filipino dailies (*Ang Pahayagang Malaya* and *Philippine Daily Inquirer*).* Three hypotheses were supported: (1) Editorials in the U.S. national prestige press would place more emphasis than those in the Philippine newspapers on topics that have evolved over a long period, received intense recent coverage and relate clearly to American interests and U.S.–Philippine relations. (2) The Philippine press would force editorials more often than the U.S. press on concrete acts and events relating to the campaign, election and revolution. (3) Editorials in either country would deal more often with acts involving primarily that country and its citizens. But the fourth hypothesis that Philippine editorials would have greater agenda diversity than American newspapers about events in the Philippines was only partially supported. Overall, the author suggests that the similarities between American and Philippine editorials tended to outweigh the differences.

> * Both *Ang Pahayagang Malaya* and *Philippine Daily Inquirer* are English daily newspapers in metro Manila of the Philippines. The former, founded in 1985, has a circulation of 165,000; whereas the latter has a circulation of 285,000.

105.

Kang, Jong Geun. 18–21 May 1987. "Newspaper Front Page Coverage of Korean Airliner Boeing 747 Massacre in Six Newspapers." Paper presented at the 78th Annual Meeting of the Eastern Communication Association held in Syracuse, New York.

> To determine the differences and direction in the coverage of the 1983 Korean Airlines (KAL) incident, the author investigated three U.S. and three foreign newspapers (*The New York Times*, *The Washington Post*, *Chicago Tribune*) and three non-U.S. newspapers (*The Times* [London], *Arab News*, and *Korea Herald*).* The sample included a total of 192 news stories between 2 and 11 September 1983. Results show: (1) There was no significant difference in the direction of the news stories among the six newspapers. (2) The percentage of news stories containing harsh descriptions of Soviet actions were significantly greater than the percentage of stories reporting only the general facts of the incident. However, it was not found that the space alloted to the story in U.S. newspapers was greater than that in non-U.S. newspapers.

> * *Arab News*, which was founded in 1975, is an English newspaper published in Jeddah, Saudi Arabia. Its circulation is 110,000. *Korea Herald*, founded in 1953, is an independent English morning newspaper in Seoul (South Korea) with a circulation of 150,000.

106.

McLeod, Douglas M. and Bob Craig. 1–4 August 1987. "Understanding Discrepancies in International News Coverage of the KAL 007 Airline Incident." Paper presented at the 70th Annual Meeting of the Association for Education in Journalism and Mass Communication held in San Antonio, Texas.

> The authors examined the influence of nation states' self-interests on their media's coverage of a major news event—the Soviet shooting down of a Korean airliner. The sample included 705 articles, broadcasts and telecasts that appeared between 1 September and 31 December 1983 in the media of 73 nations including the U.S. and the Soviet Union. Countries were subdivided into groups based on their relationships to the two superpowers. The data shows: (1) There were discrepencies between different accounts of the politically significant incident. (2) The international alignment of a news organization's nation of origin with respect

to the U.S. and the Soviet Union was reflected in the way that organization characterized the discrepant issues of the incident.

107.

Fenby, Jonathan. 1986. *The International News Services: A Twentieth Century Fund Report*. New York: Schocken Books. 275 pp.

In response to charges by Third World countries that Western news agencies monopolize international news flows, the Twentieth Century Fund commissioned this analysis of four major international news agencies: AP, UPI, Reuters and AFP. Fenby reviews the history and current role of the wire services, showing how they are structured financially and editorially and how they operate. Relevant issues discussed include the problems the agencies have covering news outside the metropolitan areas of Third World countries, the mounting Third World criticism of the agencies, alternative proposals to a New International Information Order, and the prospect for resolving this conflict between the West and the Third World.

108.

Mehra, Achal. 1986. *Free Flow of Information: A New Paradigm*. Contributions to *The Study of Mass Media and Communications*, No. 7. Westport, Conn.: Greenwood Press. 225 pp.

The author addresses the problems inherent in the international exchange of information among societies with different levels of restraint on free expression. He attempts to reconcile two seemingly incompatible positions represented by the doctrine of free flow of information on the one hand, and the New International Information Order on the other. Following an introductory overview of the free flow of information debate, the author traces the historical development of freedom of expression, examines its applicability to international information, and then charts its evolution of its fundamental principles in the United Nations. Then he examines the problems and challenges that freedom of expression poses to societies and lists some of the restraints on freedom. Finally, the author develops the philosophical basis for criticism of and restraints on freedom of expression, to attempt to reconcile the recommended restraints with the principles of free expression, and to offer practical steps the United States could take to establish a new paradigm of free flow of information.

109.

Hermano, T. Z., ed. 1985. *Communication Challenges of Our Time: An Asian Perspective.* London: Asia Region—World Association for Christian Communication. 133 pp.

This book contains the papers and reports presented at the 1984 Manila Conferences on Communication Issues and Curriculum Development. There are two parts. The papers in Part 1, which are more related to this compilation than those in Part 2, deal with communication issues, including a historical perspective on the New World Information and Communication Order (NWICO), the NWICO from the American perspective, the threat to NWICO values within religious structures, communication education related to the NWICO, a Third World view on the economic base of the NWICO, and recent mass media research related to the NWICO.

110.

Soderlund, Walter C. and S. H. Surlin, eds. 1985. *Media in Latin America and the Caribbean: Domestic and International Perspectives.* Windsor, Ontario: Ontario co-operative Programme in Latin American and Caribbean Studies, University of Windsor. 272 pp.

This volume contains 14 papers presented at a conference held at the University of Windsor on 26 and 27 October 1984. The papers in Part 1 are concerned with the New World Information Order and the MacBride Report. Part 2, on media performance in Latin America and the Caribbean, is concerned with the conceptual areas of information flow, politics, and freedom. Part 3, which is particularly relevant to this compilation, examines factors associated with how events and issues in Latin America and the Caribbean are portrayed in the North American press. Part 4 focuses on various aspects of the invasion of Grenada in October 1983, particularly coverage of the event by Western and Third World media.

111.

Stevenson, Robert L. 1985. *An Atlas of Foreign News*. Research Review No. 3. Chapel Hill, N.C.: Centre for Research in Journalism and Mass Communication, University of North Carolina.

This atlas of foreign news summarizes the results of a multinational study of foreign news organized by the International Association for Mass Communication Research (IAMCR) at the request of UNESCO. The two-week data were collected for 17 countries in all parts of the world, and for the four major Western news agencies. This atlas presents date from this project that could not be included in the individual presentations. The emphasis is on statistics rather than interpretation. Some data concerning the print media are related to Western countries' news attention to the Third World.

112.

Sreberny-Mohammadi, Annabelle, et al., eds. 1985. *Foreign News in Media: International Reporting in 29 Countries*. Reports and Papers on Mass Communication, No. 93. Paris: UNESCO. 96 pp.

This monograph reports the findings of an international research project in which 13 national teams adopted a comparative research design to cover 29 different countries.* Contents include the purpose and scope of the project, the selection and interpretation of international news, and the structure of international news reporting. Two important results, among many others, are regionalism in all international news and the identification of a particular pattern of news attention. As the scope is very broad, there is always something pertinent to the understanding of Third World coverage.

* See the note in Entry No. 27.

113.

Ahern, Thomas J., Jr. 1984. "Determinants of Foreign Coverage in U.S. Newspapers." In *Foreign News and the New World Information Order*, edited by Robert L. Stevenson and Donald Lewis Shaw, pp. 217–36. Ames, Iowa: Iowa State University Press.

The author looks at how, and how much national economic, political, social and geographical characteristics influence the international news flow into the United States. First, the author focuses on how national variables influence news flow, drawing on previous research to determine mechanisms through which such variables affect coverage. Second, seven national variables are organized into a model showing their effects on foreign news coverage. Results show that increase in trade with the U.S. is likely to produce an increase in a nation's GNP and vice versa. Increasing a nation's GNP and trade with the U.S. broadens the scope of a nation's political dialogue with the U.S. Increases in a nation's GNP, trade and scope of political dialogue, all produce increases in a nation's coverage in elite U.S. newspapers. Together these variables account for 59% of the variance in foreign coverage.

114.

Gerbner, George and Marsha Siefert, eds. 1984. *World Communications: A Handbook*. New York: Longman. 527 pp.

The first two parts of this huge volume are particularly relevant to this collection: Part I "Global Perspectives on Information" including Mustapha Masmoudi's classic call for a New World Information Order, and Part II "Transnational Communications: The Flow of News and Images" addressing a Third World concern, i.e. "who controls international news flow."

115.

Haynes, Robert D., Jr. 1984. "Test of Galtung's Theory of Structural Imperialism." In *Foreign News and the New World Information Order*, edited by Robert L. Stevenson and Donald Lewis Shaw, pp. 200–16. Ames, Iowa: Iowa State University Press.

According to Galtung's theory of structural imperialism, there exists in developing countries a dominant group whose interests coincide with the interests of the developed world. This "centre" provides a means by which the core can maintain its economic and political domination. Developing countries therefore receive information about their core but little about fellow developing countries. This test of Galtung's theory assessed the degree to which, if the core actors are defining news according to the criteria and demand for news in the developed world market, the demand for and criteria for news is similar in the centre of the peripheral nations. Analysis of the data from the UNESCO foreign news study indicated that communication flow, especially news flows, do not necessarily follow the same lines as other types of structural relations. News flows respond to cultural, linguistic and geographical determinants, rather than to the flows on investment and trade, thereby creating a situation in which periphery nations interact with other centre nations.

116.

Link, Jere H. 1984. "Test of the Cultural Dependency Hypothesis." In *Foreign News and the New World Information Order*, edited by Robert L. Stevenson and Donald Lewis Shaw, pp. 186–99. Ames, Iowa: Iowa State University Press.

The author compared the news agenda of Latin American major city dailies (two Mexican, two Brazilian, two Argentinian) with the news agenda of four international wire services (AP, UPI, Reuters and AFP). It was found that three of the four wire services had highly similar news agendas—Reuters' agenda was clearly different from those of the other three. Most of the papers showed strong agreement with the wire service agenda, but there were exceptions. The data revealed that the more sources were attributed in a newspaper, the more the newspaper tended to print a thematic agenda dissimilar to those of the wire services. This does not necessarily reflect any genuine cultural independence. The author concluded that what the Latin American press system should have a news agency for the region.

117.

Yadava, Jaswant S., eds. 1984. *Politics of News: Third World Perspectives*. New Delhi: Concept Publishing Company. 300 pp.

This collection of essays and research studies is intended to throw into relief some aspects of the debate over international news flow, highlighting the Third World point of view. The first part contains three papers which critically examine the major events in the debate and bring conceptual and ideological issues into focus. The second part contains five papers which examine foreign news coverage, especially from the Third World. The studies were done as part of an international co-operative research project carried out by thirteen national teams and covering 29 countries. The third part of the book focuses on news agencies, news pools and the distribution of the radio spectrum. Included are papers which discuss (1) conceptual and ideological issues in news production and distribution at various levels; (2) the performance of Third World news pool, with a focus on the use of the news pool by the Press Trust of India; (3) the question of Third World entry into the world market for news; and (4) the political economy of the radio spectrum and Third World interests.

118.

Nordenstreng, Kaarle. 1984. *The Mass Media Declaration of UNESCO*. Norwood, N.J.: Ablex Publishers. 475 pp.

> This book examines the 1978 Mass Media Declaration of UNESCO, not only for its historical and diplomatic implications, but primarily for its importance to the basic professional training and lifelong education of journalists. The first part of the volume reviews the international political context out of which the Declaration emerged, focusing on the debate over a "New International Information Order." The second part deals with one of the most significant consequences of the Declaration—the development of an "international law of communications." The third part deals with the consequences of the Declaration on the professional field of journalism and mass communication. Twenty-seven major documents, declarations, and other materials pertinent to the issues in the book are appended.

119.

Paraschos, Emmanuel E. 1984. "Greece and Turkey Mirrored." In *Foreign News and the New World Information Order*, edited by Robert L. Stevenson and Donald Lewis Shaw, pp. 127–32. Ames, Iowa: Iowa State University Press.

This study tested two hypotheses: (1) Each of the two press systems (Greece and Turkey) would give the other country similar play quantitatively (in number of stories, length and story type). (2) The media of each of the countries would present a negative quantitative image of the other country (in terms of topic selection, and of affect toward principal newsmakers). The largest daily in each country (*Ta Nea* in Greece and *Milliyet* in Turkey)* was examined. Coverage of Cyprus was included in the data because that country represents a unique common news target for both papers. Results showed that the Greek paper covered Turkey 60% more than the Turkish paper covered Greece, but Turkey covered Cyprus with four times as many stories as Greece covered it. The two papers treated international news in much the same way; the majority of foreign news was found in the main news section of the papers. The overall image each national paper presented of the other country was negative.

* *Ta Nea*, published in Athens (Greece), is regarded as a Western newspaper. It is a liberal evening newspaper founded in 1944 and has a circulation of 155,000. *Milliyet*, founded in Istanbul (Turkey) in 1950, is a morning newspaper with a circulation of 210,000.

120.

Stevenson, Robert L. and Donald Lewis Shaw, eds. 1984. *Foreign News and the New World Information Order*. Ames, Iowa: Iowa State University Press. 243 pp.

The recurring theme in this collection of studies is that the problems of world news flow are not so much problems of Western dominance as they are problems of journalism: the criticisms of the West can be applied to foreign coverage of every national system studied. In Part 1, papers include an overview of the issues in foreign news coverage analysis. Part 2 includes studies of contingencies in the structure of foreign news, and a comparative study of Third World elite newspapers. Part 3 contains two studies of foreign news in Western news agencies, a test of the cultural dependency hypothesis, a test of Galtung's theory of structural imperialism, and an analysis of the determinants of foreign news coverage in American newspapers.

121.

Stevenson, Robert L. and Donald Lewis Shaw. 1984. "Leaders and Conflict in the News in 'Stable' vs. 'Pluralistic' Political Systems." In *Foreign News and the New World Information Order*, edited by Robert L. Stevenson and Donald Lewis Shaw, pp. 133–47. Ames, Iowa: Iowa State University Press.

> The authors attempted to evaluate newspapers' coverage of foreign affairs in stable and pluralistic political systems. Pluralistic systems refers to countries that have adopted a relatively "pluralistic" approach to political freedoms and civil rights; stable systems are the countries that have developed more "stable" approaches to those freedoms. It was found that stable countries appeared to control the amount of conflict in the coverage of foreign affairs and to keep a strong focus on the executive as a leader. Pluralistic systems provided a wider range of news figures, had more access to them, and did not shy away from internal conflict. It is obvious that many Third World countries belong to the stable category and Western countries to the pluralistic category. The findings may have implications on the different interpretations of Third World coverage between representatives or leaders of the First and Third Worlds.

122.

Stevenson, Robert L. and Richard R. Cole. 1984. "Issues in Foreign News." In *Foreign News and the New World Information Order*, edited by Robert L. Stevenson and Donald Lewis Shaw, pp. 37–62. Ames, Iowa: Iowa State University Press.

> As the first chapter of the book, this article provides an overview of the charges about the state of world communications and the dominance of the U.S. in particular. The authors identify two separate kinds of issues— one between East and West and the other between North and South. North–South issues, which emphasize the disparity between the industrialized Western nations and the developing countries in the world, is particularly relevant to this compilation.

123.

Stevenson, Robert L. and Richard R. Cole. 1984. "Patterns of Foreign News." In *Foreign News and the New World Information Order*, edited by Robert L. Stevenson and Donald Lewis Shaw, pp. 37–62. Ames, Iowa: Iowa State University Press.

An important finding presented in this paper is that there is almost universal definition of foreign news: news is politics and foreign affairs, and newsmakers are government officials. Proximity and timeliness seem to be universal news values. The remarkable similarity between the profile of foreign news in Western news agencies and media of most countries, the authors argue, suggests that the prominence of the Western agencies is at least partly a function of their ability to provide information that can be used efficiently almost all over the world. There is no evidence supporting the allegation that news about the Third World emphasizes crises and natural disasters. The "dependence" of the Third World on Western news agencies is found to be far less pervasive than is asserted by many critics: Third World media seem uninterested in other parts of their own geographic regions and even less interested in other parts of the Third World.

124.

Stevenson, Robert L. and Gary D. Gaddy. 1984. "'Bad News' and the Third World." In *Foreign News and the New World Information Order*, edited by Robert L. Stevenson and Donald Lewis Shaw, pp. 88–97. Ames, Iowa: Iowa State University Press.

The authors divided the countries of the World into three groups—First World, Second World and Third World. For each country and news agency regional file in the sample, the researchers compared the distribution of news topics from the three Worlds using a simple Pearson correlation. A more detailed look at aspects of bad news was obtained by isolating certain main topics, and comparing the frequency with which they occurred in the media of various countries and in the news agency files. Overall, the data provided support for the argument that the Third World gets heavier coverage of bad news. About 25% of Third World news reported in all parts of the world contains some element of domestic or international conflict.

125.

Stevenson, Robert L. and J. Walker Smith. 1984. "Cultural Meaning of Foreign News." In *Foreign News and the New World Information Order*, edited by Robert L. Stevenson and Donald Lewis Shaw, pp. 98–105. Ames, Iowa: Iowa State University Press.

The authors examined differences in the coverage of Lebanon and Mexico in *Time* and *Newsweek* magazines and tried to explain the differences on the basis of cultural meanings, i.e. subjective meanings attached to the coverage in the two cultures. The aim was to see whether coverage of the two countries differs, or whether the perception of differences lies in the cultural meanings. It is not supported that these two countries are covered in mostly negative ways. Evidence shows a strong positive cultural meaning, a somewhat positive image of power, and basically a neutral coverage of activity. This is an enlightening article that attempts to shed new light on the debate of the NWIO from a cultural perspective.

126.

Stevenson, Robert L. and Kirsten D. Thompson. 1984. "'Contingencies' in the Structure of Foreign News." In *Foreign News and the New World Information Order*, edited by Robert L. Stevenson and Donald Lewis Shaw, pp. 71–87. Ames, Iowa: Iowa State University Press.

The authors employ contingency analysis to examine foreign news coverage data for the mass media of the U.S., U.S.S.R., Brazil, Algeria, and Zambia in order to identify which topics are linked to which parts of the world and which kinds of actors are linked to what topics. It was found that there was no consistency in foreign news coverage in the patterns of linkages. Overall, the U.S. media did not link the West with favourable topics and the Third World with negative topics, as has been charged. The data suggests a narrow definition of news and a limited journalistic sense of who ought to be given access to the media.

127.

Van Dijk, Teun A. 1984. *Structures of International News: A Case Study of the World's Press*. Amsterdam: University of Amsterdam, Department of General Literary Studies. 340 pp.

> This report, compiled under the auspices of the UNESCO project on the New International Information and Communication Order, presents the results of a systematic analysis of a significant international news event—the assassination of Bachir Gemayel, president-elect of Lebanon, on 14 September 1983 from a sample of the world's press.* On most structural dimensions, no major differences were found between the news items in newspapers of the First and Third Worlds, but some background categories appeared to be missing in the Third World news stories. The number of articles and the size of the coverage in these two Worlds were similar. Major differences were found in the sources from which they drew their news: the Third World press was nearly fully dependent on transnational news agencies. Western newspapers used their own correspondents to supplement wire service reports. Another major difference between various regions of the world was the implicit or explicit evaluations in the news articles and the background articles.

> * The world's press in this study included 139 newspapers from 10 different regions of the world: 5 from North America, 52 from Western Europe, 3 from Australia/ Oceania, 11 from Central America, 13 from South America, 13 from Eastern Europe, 9 from the Middle East, 13 from Africa, 5 from South Asia, 15 from East and Southeast Asia. The Western press among the top 13 newspapers that have the largest coverage of the events in Lebanon are: *The New York Times*, *Los Angeles Times*, *NRC-Handelsblad* (Netherlands), *Le Monde* (France), *Le Soir* (Belgium), *The Guardian* (United Kingdom) and *El Pais* (Spain). In terms of the size of mean newspaper coverage in different world regions, the Middle East papers naturally ranked first, followed by North America, Australia/Oceania, South America, and Western Europe, Central America, Africa, South Asia, East and Southeast Asia, and Eastern Europe.

128.

Weaver, David H. and G. Cleveland Wilhoit. 1984. "Foreign News in the Western Agencies." In *Foreign News and the New World Information Order*, edited by Robert L. Stevenson and Donald Lewis Shaw, pp. 153–85. Ames, Iowa: Iowa State Univesity Press.

> Using the coding scheme of the UNESCO study of foreign news coverage by the mass media in 17 countries, the authors examined the coverage of AP, UPI, AP wire to three Latin American countries, UPI wire to Latin America, AFP wire to Latin America, Reuters wire to Latin America, Reuters wire to the Middle East, and AFP wire to Francophone Africa. The general finding is that international wire news reporting equals politics: political and military matters make up the bulk of Western wire service reporting, leaving little space for cultural, religious, scientific and medical news. Although the data did not support the charge that the less developed countries are neglected in the foreign coverage of the two U.S. regional wire services, the findings supported the claim that Western news agencies focus on conflicts and crises when covering the less develped countries.

129.

Abel, Elie. 1983. "What Is the New World Information Order?" In *Third World News in American Media: Experience and Prospects* (Columbia Journalism Monograph, No. 4), edited by Donald Shanor and Donald H. Johnston, pp. 5–8. Columbia University.

> Abel, a member of the MacBride Commission, maintains that the New World Information Order means different things to different countries. To better understand the debate, facts should be distinguished from myth. (1) The four big international news agencies are not so immensely profitable. (2) The people of developing countries are not passive receivers of information. Then Abel mentions a few complaints by the Third World critics and responds to them. He also calls for some practical steps to reduce the communications gap between the developed and developing countries and points out that none of the Commission's recommendations—establishing newspapers and national news agencies, preferential tariffs for telecommunications between the First and Third Worlds—had been followed up.

130.

Balk, Alfred, Peter Bird Martin, Brennon Jones, Jim Anderson, Stephens Broening, et al. 1983. "New Approaches to Presenting Third World News." In *Third World News in American Media: Experience and Prospects* (Columbia Journalism Monograph, No. 4), edited by Donald Shanor and Donald H. Johnston, pp. 46–63. Columbia University.

> This is the last part of the monograph devoted to new approaches in the Third World coverage. Balk, editor of *World Press Review*, argues that efforts should be made to widen the American audiences because many alternative Third World news sources already exist. He suggests to set up a task force to discuss matters related to the improvement of Third World coverage. Jones, executive director of Interlink,* and Martin, editor-in-chief of the South–North News Service, call for the extention of an existing agency or the establishment of a new one. Jones says Interlink is needed to ensure enough Third World coverage and to trigger story ideas for the media. Martin emphasizes that Third World stories should be written by people who understand Third World cultures. Anderson, UPI diplomatic correspondent in Washington, notes that the Kuwait News Agency (KUNA),** is providing some alternate sources of information and insights about the Middle East. Broening, editor of the op-ed page of the *Baltimore Sun*, says that the growing number of op-ed pages in the U.S. could provide a wider forum for Third World views.

> * Interlink is an agency that edits news provided by Inter Press Service explicitly for the U.S. market. It attempts to meet the interest of the American audience without losing the quality of the Third World journalists' work.
> ** Kuwait News Agency (KUNA) is founded in 1976 as an independent public body. It also publishes research digests on topics of common and special interest.

131.

Bishop, Robert L. 1983. "U.S. Coverage of the Third World: A Review." In *Third World News in American Media: Experience and Prospects* (Columbia Journalism Monograph, No. 4), edited by Donald Shanor and Donald H. Johnston, pp. 15–18. Columbia University.

Bishops attempts to answer the most significant questions concerning

U.S. coverage of the Third World. Questions include: (1) How much news is available in the Third World? (2) How good a job is being done by the regional files of the international news agencies? (3) How adequate is the coverage by the wires in the U.S.? (4) How good is the coverage by broadcasting? (5) What kind of job do national and regional newspapers do? (6) How much of the news agency copy gets on the state wires? (7) What are local newspapers doing? Many of the Third World charges cannot be substantiated with empirical data.

132.

Davison, W. Phillips. 1983. "Three Audiences for Third World News." In *Third World News in American Media: Experience and Prospects* (Columbia Journalism Monograph, No. 4), edited by Donald Shanor and Donald H. Johnston, pp. 9–14. Columbia University.

Davison indicates three kinds of audience for Third World news in the U.S.—the crisis audience, the attentive public, and the specialist public. The press is to serve all of these audiences. In light of the fact that the specialist audience depends on the press for information (in addition to other specialized sources) and their importance in influencing decision-making in the country, they should be well informed by the press. As those who monitor and criticize decisions made by policy-makers in a democratic society are the attentive public, they should have enough information from the press to exercise their critical capacities. And as the crisis audience consists of taxpayers and voters, they should be informed to the extent that the public interest, however defined, is being adequately looked after. In short, the press should provide a link between these audiences. Some problems of covering Third World news are also included.

133.

Hamelink, Cees J. 1983. *Cultural Autonomy in Global Communications: Planning National Information Policy.* New York: Longman. 143 pp.

Hamelink argues that cultural autonomy is essential to independent national development. However, it is virtually impossible in a system which attempts to integrate the weak and poor countries in a global community that serves best the interest of only the rich and powerful. This autonomy has to be secured through the formulation and implementation of national policies based on international dissociation that encourages self-reliant development and co-operation of developing countries among themselves. This book is particularly relevant in Chapters 3, 4 and 5. Chapter 3 discusses resistance to cultural synchronization, focusing on the debate of the NIIO. In Chapters 4 and 5, the author argues for the incorporation of the concept of dissociation into national information policies and provides guidelines for co-operation among Third World countries.

134.

Merrill, John C. 1983. *Global Journalism: A Survey of the World's Mass Media*. New York: Longman. 374 pp.

This book deals with global journalism and mass communication by region of the world, and by special topics related to each region. Topics include problems of propaganda, world news agencies, international broadcasting, governments and the press, and worldwide journalism education. Of relevance to this collection is Part 1: The Global Perspective that deals with some conceptual problems in international communication. Merrill also elaborated on the problems of national images, global news flow, global press philosophies, and a "New Information Order" for the world.

135.

Nawaz, Shuja. 1983. "Improving U.S. Journalists Understanding: A Second View." In *Third World News in American Media: Experience and Prospects* (Columbia Journalism Monograph, No. 4), edited by Donald Shanor and Donald H. Johnston, pp. 39–43. Columbia University.

Nawaz contended that with a tendency to lump the Third World together as impoverished countries dependent on aid, Americans do not understand the Third World well enough. He criticized that American journalists lack knowledge and interest in the economic, politcal and social developments of the Third World. Without adequate preparation, American reporters simplistically transpose their own American experiences onto the Third World realities. He suggested that scholars and professionals in the Third and Western Worlds jointly organize training workshops and seminars to improve mutual understanding.

136.

Payne, Les, Nate Polowetzky, Michael Massing and Joan Dassin. 1983. "Current Patterns of Third World Coverage." In *Third World News in American Media: Experience and Prospects* (Columbia Journalism Monograph, No. 4), edited by Donald Shanor and Donald H. Johnston, pp. 22–38. Columbia University.

This is the third part of the monograph highlighting current patterns of American media coverage of the Third World. Payne, a former correspondent in Africa, suggests that Americans will not know much about important Third World developments if the U.S. sets the agenda for Third World news. Polowetzky, foreign editor of the AP, points out in-depth reporting trends in American newspapers' coverage of the Third World. Massing, contributing editor of the *Columbia Journalism Review*, finds that local correspondents working for international wire services in the Third World often report the official and safe version of the news. Dassin, professor of Fordham University, notes most American newspapers depend on wire services to define the news for them from Central America, wondering how the American readers can judge the accuracy of a story and what story is not reported.

137.

Shanor, Donald and Donald H. Johnston, eds. 1983. *Third World News in American Media: Experience and Prospects* (Columbia Journalism Monograph, No. 4), edited by Donald Shanor and Donald H. Johnston. Columbia University.

This monograph results from a conference on the flow of news between the Third and First Worlds held in May 1982 at Columbia University. It comprises 18 articles in five parts: (1) The Information Gap Controversy, (2) Will Americans Accept More Third World Information?

(3) Current Patterns of Third World Coverage, (4) Education and Training of Journalists, and (5) New Approaches to Presenting Third World News. Overall, given the context of the NWIO debate, the conference participants have offered excellent ideas and suggestions on Western media coverage of news in the Third World.

138.

Yu, Frederick T. C. 1983. "Improving U.S. Journalists' Understanding of the Third World." In *Third World News in American Media: Experience and Prospects* (Columbia Journalism Monograph, No. 4), edited by Donald Shanor and Donald H. Johnston, pp. 33–38. Columbia University.

> Yu raised crucial questions that journalism programmes must deal with in order to make American journalists more knowledgeable about the Third World: To what extent has the American press managed to keep up or adjust to changes in the world? What has the American press done to update its definition of world news, its concepts about foreign correspondence and its ideas about training of foreign correspondents? The author then proposed two sets of programmes with a dual focus on reporting and area studies. Hopefully, with adequate preparation, American journalists could appreciate Third World problems and produce the kind of news Third World representatives claim to be missing.

139.

Fenby, Jonathan. 1982. *The State of UNESCO: Background to the Information Debate*. Medford, Mass.: Edward R. Murrow Center for Public Diplomacy, Fletcher School of Law and Diplomacy, Tufts University. 25 pp.

> The United Nations system has become more polarized in recent years than at any time since the height of East–West confrontation which marked its first decade. The principal division which runs through the organization is no longer between Washington and Moscow; it stems rather from the transformation of the United Nations into a forum in which the poor nations of the world can confront the industrialized

nations of North America, Western Europe and Japan. In this monograph the author provides a chronology of the background of a major element of this confrontation: the debate over a New World Information Order, in which UNESCO has come to play a central role. The author suggests that the attention focused on the information debate has obscured the underlying nature of UNESCO, its internal balance of power, the scope of its activities, the view which it takes of itself and of its role and the relationships between the organizations and its member states.

140.

Cuthbert, Marlene. February 1981. *The Caribbean News Agency: Third World Model* (Journalism Monograph No. 71). Lexington, Ky.: Association for Education in Journalism. 41 pp.

The Caribbean is one region in the Third World where nations have banded together to improve news flow, and this resulted in the formation of the Caribbean News Agency (CANA) in 1976. In this monograph, after briefly tracing its West Indian setting, the author examines the background and the precipitating factors in the emergence of CANA during the period 1962 to 1976, describes the nature and discusses the implications of the resulting agency. Several conclusions are presented: (1) When government owns media, the formation of a regional rather than a national news agency can promote independence from governments because public ownership based on several countries minimizes the danger that any single government can exert a decisive political influence. (2) In Third World regions with limited resouces, the co-operation of institutions both internal and external to the region is likely to be necessary if a news agency is to succeed. (3) A news agency in a geographically scattered region requires extensive telecommunication facilities. (4) The Third World can provide a more indigeneous news perspective without interferring with press freedom.

141.

Hachten, William A. 1981. *The World News Prism: Changing Media, Clashing Ideologies.* Iowa State University Press. 133 pp.

Hachten first focuses on the immense technological and operational changes—communication satellites, computerization, high-speed data transfer—that continue to transform the international news media and shape a new capability for global communication. He provides insights into how and why international news communication is evolving and where it is headed. Then he analyses the problems these technological changes have intensified, problems that are rooted in the divergent political and philosophical approaches to the function and uses of mass media of the First, Second and Third Worlds. These conflicts over transnational dissemination of news and information have fuelled the continuing debate over the New World Information Order. Hachten further analyses the genesis and nature of the dispute, expanding the traditional four theories of the press into five concepts that provide a framework for understanding the controversy.

142.

Pollock, John Crothers. 1981. *The Politics of Crisis Reporting: Learning to Be a Foreign Correspondent*. New York: Praeger. 211 pp.

The author examines individual characteristics of foreign correspondents and their relationship to the correspondents' professional orientation toward analytical and adversarial reporting and "tolerant pluralism in international affairs." He concludes that foreign correspondents develop professional orientations by a gradual, incremental learning process that integrates prior experiences with their immediate social context.

143.

Richstad, Jim and Michael H. Anderson, eds. 1981. *Crisis in International News: Policies and Prospects*. New York: Columbia University Press. 473 pp.

The essays in this volume focus on the serious, emerging crisis over news collection, dissemination, and policy-making within and between nations. Part 1 presents sketches of the broad international context in which Third World countries complain about the uneven distribution of news and other communication resources. Several key concepts—domination, free flow, right to communicate, pluralism, New

International Information Order—are closely examined. Essays in Part 2 focus specifically on the debate surrounding the free and balanced flow of news within and between societies. Part 3 examines the major internationally active news agencies and addresses various news policy and practice questions that have developed around these influential organizations headquartered in a few Western industrial societies. Part 4 considers the emerging patterns of global news co-operation, news dependence and structural change, the Non-Aligned News Agencies Pool, the Western media and the Third World challenge, as well as future problems and directions on international news.

144.

Said, Edward W. 1981. *Covering Islam: How the Media and the Experts Determine How We See the Rest of the World.* New York: Pantheon Books. 186 pp.

The book focuses on both American and European perceptions of Islam and how these perceptions misguide journalists upon whom ordinary people rely to interpret political, military and economic events in the Islamic world. Comparing the coverage of Islam between European and American media, Said maintains that European reporting is more insightful and accurate. The reporters' direct experience with the Islamic world is an important factor.

145.

Sarti, I. 1981. "Communication and Cultural Dependency: A Misconception." In *Communication and Social Structure*, edited by Emile G. McAnany, et al., pp. 317–34. New York: Praeger.

The author takes issue with the "cultural dependency" approaches to Latin American society in connection with mass communication and other cultural and ideological concerns. Stressing the complexity of Latin America, she rejects the view of seeing people in developing countries as passive receivers of messages elaborated abroad and advances a view that underlines local creativity. She argues that understanding of each society's social structure should be the foundation of communication studies aimed at identifying the ways in which various social groups differ in their use and interpretation of mass media messages.

146.

Schramm, Wilbur and Erwin Atwood. 1981. *Circulation of News in the Third World: A Study of Asia.* Hong Kong: The Chinese University Press. 360 pp.

For the week of 4–10 December 1977, Schramm and Atwood analysed the local and national news content of 18 Asian daily newspapers, the content of the international wire services (AP, UPI, Reuters and AFP) delivered to Asian clients, foreign news content of 18 Asian dailies, readership of a sample of the Asian dailies, and Asian news in a sample of Third World dailies. The second part of the book related to what the wires provide and what the Asian dailies take, is particularly relevant to this compilation. The authors found that the average wire carried six out of 30 development stories, but the average Asian daily carried between one and two. In other words, the wires provided much more development stories than the Asian newspapers could use.

147.

Voices of Freedom: A World Conference of Independent News Media. 1981. Medford, Mass.: Edward R. Murrow Center for Public Diplomacy, Fletcher School of Law and Diplomacy, Tufts University. 74 pp.

This volume contains four working papers preceding a conference held at Talloires (France) in 1981. The first paper examines the politics of the "New International Information Order" communication studies, suggesting much of the criticisms of Western media for dominating the world news flow rests on inadequate research. The second paper looks at the 21st General Conference of UNESCO at Belgrade in 1980 and concludes that the first order of business for Western media is to make clear to UNESCO that its involvement with the content of news media is incompatible with the notion of a free flow of information. The final paper explains the purpose and development of the UNESCO-sponsored International Programme for the Development of Communication (IPDC).

148.

Bielenstein, D., ed. 1980. *Toward a New World Information Order: Consequences for Development Policy.* Bonn: Friederick-Ebert-Stiftung. 114 pp.

> This volume collects working papers from a group of 80 media policy-makers, experts and journalists who met at a conference in Bonn in December 1978. The first paper provides a good summary of the debate on the establishment of a New International Information Order. Other relevant papers include Mustapha Masmoudi's elaboration on information as a social necessity, the tenets and policies of the NWIO, the German view of its consequences in terms of development co-operation, and the findings and recommendations of the conference.

149.

Boyd-Barrett, Oliver. 1980. *The International News Agencies.* Beverly Hills, Calif.: Sage Publications.

> The author talks about how the international news agencies (Tass, the Non-Aligned News Agencies Pool and Inter Press Service, especially the "big four"—AP, UPI, Reuters and AFP) work in gathering and disseminating world news. Considerable attention is also given to the conflict between developing countries and the wire services over "balance" of coverage and freedom of the press.

150.

Harris, Phil, Harald Maltczek and Ertugrul Ozkok. 1980. *Flow of News in the Gulf* (New Communication Order: No. 3). UNESCO. 69 pp.

> The authors examined the content and volume of news exchanged between the Gulf region and Europe. Complete files of the transmission of the Gulf News Agency (GNA) member news agencies (Iraq, Kuwait, Qatar, Saudi Arabia, United Arab Emirates) are collected for one week between 10 and 16 October 1978 and analysed in Bahrain. Results show: (1) An average of 1,920 lines of news per day was supplied the GNA, and of this, the GNA transmitted an average of 329 lines per day. (2) The news flowing through the GNA largely originated in the Gulf region.

(3) The news is dominated by political/military and economic news items. (4) The news is largely concentrated on domestic or bilateral events. (5) News of Arab-European interest tends to be used when events take place in Arab nations. A second analysis of the flow of information between the Gulf states, Iran and Turkey reveals the Turkish media are dependent on a few big international agencies.

151.

Hudson, Michael C. and R. G. Wolfe, eds. 1980. *The American Media and the Arabs* (*CCAS Studies in Arab–American Relations*). Washington, D.C.: Center for Contemporary Arab Studies, Georgetown University. 105 pp.

The papers in this collection discuss various elements which combine to form American opinion on the Middle East and create the popular image of the Arabs as seen through the various news media and the entertainment industry. Topics include practices, heritage and constraints of American journalism in covering the Middle East, American media perspectives on the Arab world, images and realities of the Middle East conflict, and UNESCO and the New International Information Order.

152.

MacBride, Sean, et al. 1980. *Many Voices, One World.* New York: United Nations Publications. 312 pp.

This volume, which is based on the final report of the International Commission for the Study of Communication Problems,* presents in its first four sections a survey of contemporary communication systems at the local, national, regional and international levels, focusing on economic and industry infrastructures, disparities in system developments, flaws in communication flows, dominance in communication contents, the democratization of communication, communication policies, the contribution of research to communication processes and policy, professionals in communication, the right and responsibilities of journalists, and the norms of professional conduct. The final section contains conclusions and recommendations of the Commission.

* See the note in Entry No. 61.

153.

Pollock, John Crothers and C. L. Guidette. 1980. "Mass Media, Crisis, and Political Change: A Cross-National Approach." In *Communication Yearbook 4*, edited by Dan Nimmo, pp. 309–24. New Brunswick, N.J.: Transaction Books.

> Industrial world media have been critiqued for reporting on the Third World in a uniform way and for reflecting home country economic interests. Comparing coverage in *The New York Times* and *The Times* (London), the authors discovered substantially different perspectives on crises in Brazil (1964), Chile (1970) and South Africa (1979). All three "critical events" varied substantially in the nature of their political transitions, in political direction and in economic stakes. However, consistent patterns emerge within each paper. Compared to *The New York Times*, *The Times* (London) displays a broader range of sources, presented more stable coverage, and legitimizes social change more generously. The authors conclude that microscopic, "individual" level and macroscopic, "cultural" level factors cannot account for these disparate patterns and suggest a "middle-level" explanation: distinct national strategic contexts. The authors urge that scholars focus on the pre-crisis, prior socialization of foreign correspondents to learn how journalists acquire collective professsional perspective on reporting.

154.

Smith, Anthony. 1980. *The Geopolitics of Information: How Western Culture Dominates the World*. New York: Oxford University Press. 192 pp.

> The first chapter of the book on the Old International Information Order (OIIO) provides excellent background for understanding the context of the NWIO debate. In the rest of the chapters, Smith discusses the media and news imperialism, a new international electronic order, cultural dependence, and double standards of freedom. His keen perceptions of information dissemination shed much light on how the Western culture dominates the world.

155.

Fascell, Dante B., ed. 1979. *International News: Freedom Under Attack*. Beverly Hills: Sage. 320 pp.

> Fascell, a U.S. congressman who heads the House Foreign Affairs Committee, ardently defends the free flow of news and information in the Third World. Parts particularly relevant to this compilation include: (1) Mass Media and the Third World Challenge of Part II, which discusses at length the controversial activist role of UNESCO in trying to change the pattern of international news flow and in advocating national communication policies; and (2) International News and the American Media of Part III, which deals with topics such as the definition of international news, problems of Third World coverage, and American journalism and closed societies.

156.

Fisher, Glen. 1979. *American Communication in a Global Society*. Norwood, N.J.: Ablex. 165 pp.

> This book summarizes the issues that have been argued at UNESCO and elsewhere since the mid-1970s. Fisher, an experienced foreign service officer, attempts to present an agenda for approaching the complex debate on a New World Information Order. Acknowledging many of the complaints about the dominance of Western influence in world communications, he argues that the charge of U.S. dominance or cultural imperialism is too simplistic and far-fetched. However, he calls on Americans and American institutions to be more sensitive to other people and nations which have to contend with the overpowering presence of the U.S.

157.

Nordenstreng, Kaarle and Herbert Schiller. 1979. *National Sovereignty and International Communication*. Norwood, N.J.: Ablex. 286 pp.

> Nordenstreng and Schiller, distinguished critical scholars in mass communication, see international communication flow as part of the larger struggle to break the domination of the world capitalist system. The concept of national sovereignty, which primarily refers to the right of a

nation to evolve its own communication system without external interference, is adopted to unify perspective in analysing national development. They argue the corporate properties stratum of the Western world
in the global market system determines the content of media flows and
threatens the national sovereignty of Third World countries. The authors
contribute to the debate on news flow from a Marxist perspective,
indirectly shedding light on the issue of Western press coverage of the
Third World.

158.

Tiffen, Rodney. 1978. *The News from Southeast Asia: The Sociology of
Newsmaking*. Singapore: Institute of Southeast Asian Studies. 206 pp.

Tiffen examines how career patterns, organizational demands, news
values, source structures, government attitudes and activities affect the
foreign correspondents' work. Contending that the coverage of the world
by transnational news agencies has usually been adequate, complete and
prolific, he notes that criticisms of ignorance, sporadic and crisis journalism are not applicable to news agencies. A degree of superficiality
and selectivity is built into the news agencies' work, partly because
foreign correspondents are assigned to cover large complex areas for an
audience with limited knowledge and interest. The problem is enhanced
by the orientation of these correspondents to Western news values. Thus,
while many Asian countries suffer from poverty and underdevelopment,
they have not received serious and sustained attention in the Western
press. Overall, the author has offered good reasons for the imbalanced
and inadequate coverage of developing countries in Asia.

Part III

Dissertations and Theses

159.

Guirguis, Sonia Adly. 1988. "The Image of Egypt in *The New York Times* 1956, 1967, 1979." Ph.D. dissertation, New York University. 328 pp.

> This study tests the validity of the political theory of the presentation of news through a comparative analysis of the image of Egypt presented by *The New York Times* and U.S.–Egypt government relations in three time periods: the Suez Crisis of 1956, the Egyptian–Israeli War of 1967 and the Egyptian–Israeli Peace Treaty of 1979. To determine the extent to which changes in the projected image of Egypt were similar to or different from changes in U.S.–Egypt government relations, the image of Egypt and U.S.–Egypt government relations were classified into: negative, tilted toward the negative, balanced, tilted toward the positive, and positive. Results for Time Period I indicated that the image of Egypt and U.S.–Egypt government relations were tilted toward the negative before the event, and tilted toward the positive after the event. Only during the event did the image of Egypt neither parallel nor entirely deviate from U.S.–Egypt government relations. The image of Egypt was balanced, while the U.S.–Egypt governemnt relations were tilted toward the positive. In Time Period II, they were both negative before, during and after the event; and in Time Period III, they were both positive before, during and after the event. Overall, the results support the political theory of the presentation of news, since changes in the projected image of Egypt were, to a large extent, similar to changes in U.S.–Egypt government relations.

160.

Ismail, Bukhory Bin. 1988. "Analysis of International News Coverage of 24 Nations by the United States Newspapers." Ph.D. dissertation, Ohio University. 193 pp.

> The author analysed coverage related to 24 Asian countries in *The New York Times*, *The Washington Post*, *Los Angeles Times*, and *The Christian Science Monitor*. Theme, volume, and sources of information were examined. Content Analysis was used for the first segment of the two-part study, which also included a correlational analysis between

coverage (frequency and volume) and several non-media factors: trade, population, communication, culture and dependency of the countries covered. It was found that 28.7% of international news coverage in the four papers dealt with Asian countries and Asian news coverage was mostly non-crisis oriented (73.3%). In addition, there was a positive correlation between newspaper coverage and a country's level of trade, but no correlation between coverage and a nation's level of dependency was found.

161.

Li, Sunny Tszesun. 1988. "A Comparative Study of Reciprocal Coverage of the People's Republic of China in *The Washington Post* and the United States in *People's Daily* in 1986: A Case Study of Foreign News within the Context of the Debate of the New World Information Order." Ed.D. dissertation, Oklahoma State University. 202 pp.

This study content analysed *The Washington Post*'s coverage of China and *People's Daily*'s* coverage of the U.S. in 1986. In examining the nature of foreign news, it intended to assess some of the Third World allegations of the Western media in the debate of the New World Information Order on a reciprocal basis, applying the same standards of evaluation across the two media systems. Findings include: (1) *People's Daily* devoted significantly more attention in terms of the number of items, space and attention scores than *The Washington Post* to reciprocal coverage; however, the *Post* fared significantly better in attention on an item-to-item basis. (2) There was as much difference as similarity between the topical patterns of the two newspapers. (3) The degree of thematic negativism in reciprocal coverage was similar across the two systems; however, reciprocal attention to certain categories of negative and positive themes was quite different. (4) The vast majority of items in both papers tended to be neutral. (5) The *Daily* was as "independent" (from the influence of non-national sources) as the *Post*. Nevertheless, the *Daily* was heavily "dependent" on the NCNA; only 21.5% of items were furnished by the paper. (6) The *Daily* covered more geographical locations in which stories happened than the *Post*; however, coverage of the geographical regions and the kinds of people of each other's country were equally imbalanced.

* *People's Daily (Renmin Ribao)*, founded in 1948 as the organ of the Chinese Communist Party, has a circulation of 5 million. It also publishes an overseas edition.

162.

Al-Karni, Ali A. 1987. "Mass Media and Social Conflict: A Comparative Content Analysis of the Austin (Minnesota) Strike and the Egyptian Food Riots." Ph.D. dissertation, University of Minnesota. 178 pp.

Reporting social conflict is a direct function of the relationships that link the mass media subsystem to other powerful institutions in society. This study examines differences across systems in the way media report social conflict, particularly conflict between the political-economical establishment and other opposing social groups. The Austin Hormel Strike (1985–1987) and the Egyptian Food Crisis (1977) are selected for their representations of conflicts in more and less pluralistic societies. Results suggest that as the conflict proceeds, the tendency is to give more "position" news statements to the establishment groups than to the protest groups, and more "action" news statements to the protest groups than to the establishment groups. The tendency, in both systems, is to show institutional (third parties) rejection to changes desired by the protest groups. The rejection is transferred into dissemination of negative images about the movements, which aim at delegitimizing the issues and actors of movements.

163.

Sadeghi, Mansour. 1987. "National Differences and International Crisis Reporting: A Gatekeeper Study of the 1985 TWA Hostage Crisis." Ph.D. dissertation, University of Southern California.

The purpose of this study was to determine how media gatekeepers in different countries with different values and social and political systems reported an indentical news event—the 1985 TWA Hostage Crisis—to their public. Five newspapers—*Los Angeles Times* (U.S.), *Jerusalem Post* (Israel), *Excelsior* (Mexico), *Kayhan* (Iran), and *Pravda** (Soviet Union)—were analysed. Four hypotheses were tested: (1) Newspaper gatekeepers in the United States and its ally Israel devoted more space to the TWA hostage story than did a relatively neutral country such as

Mexico and the two non-aligned nations, the Soviet Union and Iran. (2) The media gatekeepers of the U.S. and its ally Israel devoted more space in their front pages to the TWA hostage story than did a relatively neutral nation such as Mexico and the two non-aligned nations, the Soviet Union and Iran. (3) The photos that a newspaper published about the TWA hostage crisis support their political and social viewpoints. (4) In reporting the TWA hostage crisis, newspaper gatekeepers choose certain words that support their own political and social viewpoints. Results indicated the three hypotheses were supported.

* As Jerusalem is an ally of the U.S.A., The *Jerusalem Post* is regarded as a Western newspaper. It is an independent English morning newspaper founded in 1932 with circulations of 30,000 (weekdays) and 50,000 (weekend edition). Its weekly international edition has a circulation of 60,000 in 95 countries. *Excelsior*, founded in 1917, is an independent morning newspaper with a circulation of 200,000 in Mexico. *Kayhan* (Universe), founded in 1941, is an evening newspaper with an emphasis on politics in Teheran, Iran. *Pravda* (Truth), founded in Moscow in 1912 as the organ of the Central Committee of the Communist Party (CCCP) of the Soviet Union, has a circulation of 9,664,000. It is also printed in 44 major cities in the U.S.S.R.

164.

Chang, Tsan-kuo. 1986. "The News and U.S.–China Policy, 1950–1984: Relationships with the Government and Public Opinion." Ph.D. dissertation, University of Texas at Austin.

The author published an article based on this dissertation in *Journalism Quarterly*. See Entry No. 2 in Part I.

165.

El Zein, Hassan Mohamed. 1986. "*New York Times*' Coverage of Africa: A Descriptive Analysis of the Period 1976–1986." Ph.D. dissertation, Ohio University. 129 pp.

This study investigates the volume and nature of coverage of the news of the African continent in *The New York Times* in three selected years: 1976, 1981 and 1985. Results show that *The New York Times* devoted 18.06% of its total international news coverage in 1976 to the news of Africa. In 1981 the percentage was 15.05, and in 1985 it was 19.03%.

News coverage was also highly concentrated. Out of a total of 51 nations, only 25 got coverage and out of that, five seemed to dominate the coverage, namely Angola, Egypt, South Africa, Rhodesia and Libya. On page one, crisis themes comprised about 76% to 93% of the total coverage throughout the three years of study. Analysis of the front page showed that mostly crises and negative news are the categories that find space in the front page of the paper. On the whole, this study shows that despite the debate on international news flow and coverage, *The New York Times* maintains a relatively steady volume of news reporting from Africa. The crisis orientation in news reporting has been steadily increasing throughout the years of study. The study concludes with suggestions for improving the coverage of Africa in the Western media.

166.

Chang, Christin. 1985. "News Coverage of the People's Republic of China by *The New York Times*: A 1975–1982 Content Analysis." Master thesis, Iowa State University.

This study investigates how *The New York Times* reported the People's Republic of China before and after normalization with the U.S. The years of 1975 and 1982 are chosen for analysis. All six hypotheses are supported: Before and after normalization differences exist in (1) type of item covered, (2) amount of coverage (in column inches), (3) subject matter, (4) news sources, (5) usage of articles written by staff members or supplied by international news agencies, and (6) direction toward the PRC.

167.

Fridrikson, Lianne. 1984. "Coverage of Scandinavia in U.S. News Media." Master thesis, University of Texas at Austin.

The media of developed nations of the West, particualrly those in the U.S., have been charged with presenting crisis-oriented news and giving too little attention to social processes and development of the less developed countries. This thesis sought to determine whether Scandinavian countries can legitimately register similar complaints. The author examined three U.S. television networks, three U.S. news magazines and two elite U.S. newspapers and concluded that the Third World has no exclusive rights to these complaints. Crisis-oriented news items are prevalent in the reportage of Scandinavia and its overall coverage was so scant as to be practically non-existent.

168.

Kirat, Mohamed. 1984. "The Flow of International News in the Associated Press, United Press International and the Non-Aligned News Agencies Pool." Master thesis, Indiana University.

The author, together with his thesis adviser David Weaver, published an article based on this thesis in *Gazette*, 1985. See Entry No. 18 in Part I.

169.

Lalehparvaran, Parvin. 1984. "A Content Analysis of *The New York Times* and *St. Louis Post-Dispatch* Coverage of the Arab-Israeli Conflict from June 6, 1982 to February 12, 1983." Ed.D. dissertation, Oklahoma State University.

This study concerned the news coverage of Arabs and Israelis before, during and after the Beirut Massacre in *The New York Times* and *St. Louis Post-Dispatch*. The author used 40 key symbols pertaining to the conflict for analysis. They were coded according to predication: strength-plus, morality-plus, strength-minus, morality-minus and neutral. Three-way frequency analyses were conducted, juxtaposing parties to the conflict, the two papers and symbols direction. It is found that before the Massacre there are more favourable than unfavourable symbols about Israelis in both papers. During the Massacre, *The New York Times* and *St. Louis Post-Dispatch* present more favourable symbols about Arabs. As for Israelis, more favourable symbols are found in the *Times* during this phase, and the *Post-Dispatch* carries equally positive and negative symbols on Israelis. After the Massacre, both papers presented Arabs in a positive context and Israelis in the negative. Overall not enough background is provided in either paper.

170.

Ramaprased, Jyotika. 1984. "Foreign Policy and Press Coverage: A

Study of *The New York Times'* Coverage of India from 1973 to 1980."
Ph.D. dissertation, Southern Illinois University at Carbondale.

This study analysed *The New York Times'* coverage of India between
1973 and 1980, a period characterized by subtle U.S. foreign policy
changes toward India. Its purpose was to explore the relationship between news coverage and U.S. foreign policy toward India. The author
studied the trends in the length and prominence of coverage for both bias
and topic categories. The hypothesis was that the coverage of favourable
topic news would be larger and more prominent in favourable foreign
policy periods than in unfavourable foreign policy periods and vice
versa. But the study did not support this hypothesis.

171.

Bruce, Susan E. 1983. "The New World Information Order." Master's
thesis, University of Florida.

The author discusses some major issues concerning the New World
Information Order (NWIO) that include the function and control of the
media, information flow and news agencies, cultural identity and imperialism, computers and data flow, protection of journalists, and the
1980 MacBride Report. She surveys 20 members of the Brazilian media,
government communications officials and professors on the NWIO, and
finds that opinions are mixed. She concludes that UNESCO is an appropriate forum for the NWIO discussion, suggesting less hyperbole in
the rhetoric of all camps, more coverage but less one-sided approach
toward the coverage of the issues.

172.

Conway, Neil Griffith. 1983. "Foreign Correspondents' Opinion of
Foreign News in the U.S. Media." Master's thesis, University of
Maryland.

The quantity and quality of foreign news in the U.S. media have been
criticized over the past decade. These criticisms include: (1) too little
coverage of broad news; (2) even less coverage to Third World news; (3)
concentration on crises and negative events; and (4) domination of world
news by the international news agencies. This study seeks to explore the

extent to which these criticisms are reflected in the opinions of foreign correspondents working in Washington, D.C. It also tries to discover the differences in opinion toward U.S. foreign news between First and Third World correspondents. It was found that the correspondents have a favourable opinion of the accuracy and objectivity of U.S. foreign news in general, although they agree with many current criticisms. Both the First and the Third World correspondents have a high regard for the professionalism of the U.S. media, yet they feel that the media do not devote enough coverage to their countries. In their opinion, the U.S. media tend to favour foreign news stories that reflect U.S. interests, and neglect those that are mainly of interest to foreign countries themselves. It is suggested that U.S. foreign coverage displays a lack of understanding of life in foreign countries, presenting instead an American perception of it. On the whole, the findings imply that foreign correspondents find U.S. foreign news to be "accurate" but "distorted."

173.

Hutzell, Richard W. 1983. "An Examination of the New World Information Order." Master's thesis, University of Tennessee-Knoxville.

Hutzell examined some of the issues surrounding the New World Information Order. Third World critics complain that international channels of communication are biased in favour of technical and economic wealth. Western critics of the order, on the other hand, accuse its proponents of using its arguments to justify denying the people of the developing countries the right to freedom of information. The author content analysed three newspapers in Nigeria to test the charges of whether the developing countries are confronting a flood of information, particularly from the Western developed countries. It was found that the papers do not reprint automatically the information circulated by the West.

174.

Roberts, John William. 1983. "New World Information Order: Perspectives and Solutions." Master's thesis, Central Missouri State University.

The author adopts historical methods to examine the origins of the New World Information Order and the positions of the Third and Western worlds on the issue. He points out the domination of Western media systems in the international flow and the conditions that caused the information imbalances are very much in evidence. Hence, regarding the imbalanced flow as the source of cultural dilution and disunity as well as religous, tribal and ethnic conflicts, Third World representatives demand a global communications system that will allow them to use communication for vital developmental purposes. However, their Western counterparts upholds the concept of free flow of information, rejecting any attempt to establish international codes or laws that will limit the movement or access of journalists to information. Some solutions to the problem are offered at the end of the thesis.

175.

Al-Karni, Ali A. 1982. "The Middle East in the Front Pages of Three Leading American Newspapers from 1970 to 1980." Master's thesis, Ohio University.

The author examines how the American press (*The New York Times*, *The Washington Post*, and *The Wall Street Journal*) cover the Middle East and how coverage of Israel compares with coverage of the Arab states from 1970 to 1980. Twelve issues of each paper were drawn randomly for each year. Israel received more coverage and more favourable coverage than any other Middle East country, with 127 stories, 32% of which were favourable; Egypt received the most coverage of any of the Arab states. *The Wall Street Journal* had the most stories about the Middle East, with 258, compared to 139 for the *Times*, and 135 for the *Post*. However, both the *Times* and the *Post* had nearly twice as much space devoted to the Middle East as *The Wall Street Journal* did, which indicated their stories were much longer. Overall, the number of stories about the Middle East increased from 1970 to 1980.

176.

M'Bayo, Ritchard H. 1982. "American Press Coverage of Africa, 1960–1979." Master's thesis, Howard University.

This thesis examines three U.S. magazines' (*Business Week, Time, U.S. News & World Report*) coverage of African nations and their leaders. It attempts to determine the extent of coverage of African affairs and the kind of images of Africa these magazines portray. It is also concerned with how these images have changed over time, and with the extent to which coverage varies among the three magazines. The study covers a period of 20 years (1960–1979) from which a random sample of issues of the magazines was drawn. There are three units of analysis—one contextual unit (the article), and two recording units (the country and the leader). For each unit of analysis, a set of categories designed to extract intra-media data about African nations and African leadership attributes is constructed. The author finds a negative image of Africa and whether the coverage is crisis-oriented depends largely on how crisis is defined.

177.
Ndipnchot, Martha Arrey. 1982. "A Comparative Content Analysis of News of Black Africa in Two Georgia Newspapers." Master's thesis, University of Georgia.

This study is concerned with charges of Third World critics on the coverage of their countries by the Western press. The author attempts to ascertain the extent of truth or falsity of these charges in the context of black Africa by comparatively content analysing *The Atlanta Constitution* and *Atlanta Daily World* from 1 January 1979 to 31 December 1980. It was found that the two papers correlate highly in their use of black African news by subject matter, but not as highly in the same news by geographical area or country. Unlike the *Daily World*, the *Constitution* carries more news which portrays Africa as a politically, socially and economically disorganized region. Nevertheless, the *Constitution*'s approach to news coverage is more process-oriented (i.e. shows more continuity and gives more background information) and less event-centred (i.e., shows less continuity in coverage and less background information) than that of the *Daily World*. The author argues that this difference is due more to the *Daily World*'s smaller bulk than to an attempt by the paper to present an incomplete picture of the subcontinent. Thus the Third World charge of a preponderance of negative and

inadequate news of their countries in Western media is confirmed to a
certain extent.

178.

Shah, Hemant G. 1982. "News Coverage of the New World Information
Order: A Content Analysis of Five U.S. Elite Newspapers." Master's
thesis, Purdue University.

The New World Information Order (NWIO) involves a wide range of
issues ranging from direct broadcast satellites to journalistic freedom to
the activities of Western press organizations in developing countries.
This study examined how five U.S. elite newspapers* cover the NWIO
issue between 1970 and 1980. Four research objectives were formulated
to determine the amount of coverage given to the NWIO in relation to
NWIO-related activity, the trends in the coverage given the NWIO, the
image of the NWIO as presented by the papers, and the trends in the
image of the NWIO presented in the papers. A correlation analysis was
conducted on "attention scores" (an index measuring news coverage)
and NWIO-related activity variables to determine the relationship
between newspaper coverage and NWIO-related activity. A content
analysis of 150 NWIO-related items from five U.S. papers was conducted to determine the image of the NWIO presented by them. The
results indicate that the majority of the coverage given to the NWIO by
the U.S. papers is between 1976 and 1980, that the papers concentrate on
aspects of the NWIO that relate to the press to the exclusion of other
equally important aspects of the NWIO and that the U.S. press is reluc-
tant to present a favourable image of the NWIO issue.

* The five newspapers are: *The New York Times, The Washington Post, Chicago
  Tribune, Los Angeles Times* and *The Christian Science Monitor.*

179.

Sides, Ann Bardsley. 1982. "'Darkest Africa': Toward Better Coverage
of Third World News." Master's thesis, University of Florida.

Coverage of African news by American newspapers is sparse and
focuses predominantly on wars, coups, politics, and the activities of
political leaders. There are many reasons for this pattern of coverage—

cultural differences, overlooked correspondents, the highly competitive nature of U.S. journalism and the Western definition of "news" applied to foreign events. This thesis argues that what is needed is not a New World Information Order but an approach to coverage that applies the same values and standards to foreign news as to news from the newspaper's own hometown. Foreign correspondents should be required to know the history, culture and values of the foreign communities they cover as thoroughly as they know their own community. The definition of foreign news should be broadened beyond politics and conflict to include culture, religion, business, economics and agriculture, and should include the commonplace events that add meaning or insight as well as those which are dramatic and shocking. Attention should be given to the concerns and opinions of common people in order to gain as balanced a view of foreign societies as we have of our own. To demonstrate how this concept may be applied, the author studied the coverage of Africa in five elite American newspapers* over a five-year period, using examples that best meet the "hometown" standard as an anthology.

* The five elite U.S. newspapers are: *The New York Times*, *The Washington Post*, *Los Angeles Times*, *The Christian Science Monitor* and *The Wall Street Journal*.

180.

Venker, Teresa. 1982. "U.S. Press Treatment of El Salvador, 1980–82: Primary Sources and Messages." Master's thesis, University of Wisconsin.

The author content analysed the coverage of El Salvador in *The New York Times* and *The Washington Post* from 1980 to 1982 to determine primary sources of information and messages. It was found that 51% of 1,312 identified sources were government and military officials. The author categorized 24 messages, out of which negative opinions directed toward the government were the primary kinds of statements. Over the 24-month period, there were neither major changes in who are being consulted nor in the frequency of particular statements. However, when the coverage between the first and second years was compared, criticism of the U.S. government increased substantially during the second year in which charges by U.S. officials of Communist-influenced insurgency became prominent. Covering in the second year also dropped drastically and remained low after U.S. officials publicly criticized the media's coverage of El Salvador. Reporters rarely consulted American and Salvadoran business people, ordinary residents and scholars. Most of the factual information was related to news of violence, military and political information. The study concluded that more sources, economic, social information and historical background should be included in the coverage of El Salvador in order to give a broader and more detailed picture to both the public and U.S. policy-makers of a Latin American culture in turmoil.

181.

Windham, Henry David. 1982. "A Content Analysis of International News in Mississippi Daily Newspapers." Master's thesis, University of Mississippi.

This study examined the coverage of international news in daily newspapers in Mississippi. The results show that the Mississippi daily press focused on the Middle East, printing mostly negative news. News focused on subject categories of war and defense, government acts and economic activity. More than two-thirds of the international news items were coded as negative. The percentages of positive and negative news items varied among the newspapers, but all newspapers published more negative than positive news items. Editorial page items usually dealt with politics and government acts. Features and photographs were human-interest oriented.

182.

Ahern, Thomas Joseph, Jr. 1981. "Determinants of Foreign News Coverage in Elite U.S. Newspapers." Master's thesis, Univesity of North Carolina at Chapel Hill.

The author published an article based on this thesis in *Foreign News and the New World Information Order* in 1984. See Entry No. 113 in Part II.

183.

Babbili, Anantha Sudhaker. 1981. "International News Flow and the

Non-Aligned Nations: The Predicament of Imbalance and the Right to Communicate." Ph.D. dissertation, University of Iowa.

This dissertation conceptualized the democratization of the international news flow, with particular reference to Third World countries as equal participants in the collection and dissemination of news. The study described the problem of imbalance in the international news flow and explained the origins of the political debate in light of what was new in post-World War II international relations. Particularly, it examined the aspects of power and the status quo in international relations alongside Third World nationalism expressed through non-aligned foreign policy as decisive factors in the debate. The practicality of political solutions offered by Western, Socialist and Third World countries to redress the problems was also examined. Finally, the author called for an alternative model of international news which was centred on cultural diversity—a sensitivity to needs and aspirations of Third World nations. Within that perspective, the author suggested some broad policy recommendations concerning both structural components of the model and desired changes in news values and journalistic professionalism.

184.

Cline, Carolyn Garrett. 1981. "Our Neglected Neighbours: How the U.S. Elite Media Covered Latin America in 1977." Ph.D. dissertation, Indiana University.

Cline examined the coverage of Latin America by the American elite media—three news magazines (*Time*, *Newsweek* and *U.S. News & World Report*) for 1977 and seven newspapers (*The New York Times*, *The Washington Post*, *The Wall Street Journal*, *Chicago Tribune*, *Los Angeles Times*, *The Christian Science Monitor*, and *The Miami Herald*) for a constructed month and the network news broadcasts of ABC, NBC and CBS. Three hypotheses were supported: (1) Latin American news was reported less than news from other world areas. (2) "Official" news of business or dipolmacy dominated the coverage. (3) The average story from Latin America was shorter than the average foreign story. Given the context of the debate of the NWIO, the author concluded: While the elite media coverage of Latin America was not as bad as earlier critics said, it still needs to be improved.

185.

Morgan, Rosalyn Rolon. 1981. "Iranian News in Two Elites: *New York Times* and *Le Monde*, 1977–79." Master's thesis, University of Missouri.

> This study compared the coverage of Iran in *The New York Times* (U.S.) and *Le Monde* (France). Two research questions were asked: Does *Le Monde* with its analytical participatory role, predict events, critique American foreign policy and reflect little cultural bias toward Third World countries? Does *The New York Times* with its reactive, objectively neutral role, provide little prediction, critique foreign policy less and exhibit more cultural bias? It was found that the *Times* dealt with the Iranian story seriously and at great length. Compared to *Le Monde*, the *Times'* coverage was massive; the paper gave the view of the U.S. on the issue. Despite differences, the two newspapers performed quite similarly—they have nearly equivalent numbers of some categories of sources; their headline directions (in the last two phrases) were almost identical and they gave most emphasis to the same two contextual variables. However, in the *Times*, the stories were more U.S.-oriented; in *Le Monde*, they included human rights violations in Iran, a major cause of the revolution, and anti-Americanism. In the measures of accountability, the *Times* was less accountable than *Le Monde*—roughly one third of the *Times'* stories contained no sources, no identified reporter, no dateline or used no U.S. officials as sources. The author concluded that the analytical *Le Monde* stressed ideas, cause-and-effect relationships and predictions while the news-oriented *Times* presented an impressive array of current events with little context. While the *Times* put events in context, it did so later, in most instances, after the fact.

186.

Mousa, Issam Suleimn. 1981. "The Arab Portrayal: *The New York Times* 1917–1947." Ph.D. dissertation, University of Washington.

> The author examined the image of Arabs in *The New York Times* from 1917 (the time when modern Arab history began) to 1947. Every third year was represented by the paper's coverage during the even-numbered days of March. To allow for the observation of trends, eleven time

periods were examined. The Arab image was examined across nine major categories: Arab referents, kind of relationship, parties in relationship in Arabs, relationship contexts, content of attributions, direction, type of attribution, general source, and specific source. It was found that coverage was primarily event-oriented, conflict-oriented, unfavourable, possibly biased in its limited contexts, and provided first by European sources which were later superceded by Arab–American–Jewish sources in the 1940s. Over this period, news focus shifted from a romanticized portrayal to one centred on conflict. The author concluded that limited coverage coupled with imbalanced information could have contributed to misconceptions about the Arabs prior to 1948 that might have aided in creating stereotypes and distortions.

187.

Azzi, Abderrahmane. 1980. "A Comparison of the Reporting of International News in Two Algerian and Two United States Daily Newspapers." Master's thesis, North Texas State University.

The author compared international world news coverage between two Algerian newspapers (*El-Moudjahid* and *Al-Doumhouria*)* and two U.S. newspapers (*The New York Times* and *The Christian Science Monitor*) in terms of type and tension. It was concluded that the four papers were similar in the type of news; they reported more news than editorials, more straight news than in-depth reports, and more news of elites than common people. In addition, contrary to a Third World complaint of little coverage, there was more news from the Third World than from the Western World. However, the tension within international news was higher in the two U.S. papers than in the Algerian papers.

* *El-Moudjahid* (The Fighter) is an Algerian newspaper founded in 1965 with a circulation of 392,000. *Al-Doumhouria* (The Republic), another Algerian newspaper, is founded in 1963. Its circulation is around 70,000.

188.

Hadjipavlou, Maria Constantinou. 1980. "*The New York Times* Coverage of the 1974 Cyprus Crisis, 16–26 July 1974." Master's thesis, University of Kansas.

The author studied *The New York Times*' coverage of the 1974 Cyprus crisis from the 16–26 of July 1974. It was found that the *Times* covered extensively all events during the crisis. In its editorials it stood against the coup and the Turkish invasion and called for the speedy implementation of the United Nation's resolution on Cyprus. It was concluded that the coverage was analytical, detailed and often prophetic with few omissions or signs of bias, and that such coverage can serve as a valuable document and source for the foreign correspondent who is interested in telling the truth about a foreign event.

189.

Husni, Samir. 1980. "A Content Analysis of Press Coverage of the 1975–76 Lebanese Civil War by *The New York Times* and *The Times* of London." Master's thesis, North Texas State University.

This study examined the extent of coverage in total wordage, the direction and intensity of coverage, and the attitude toward the main parties of the war in *The New York Times* and *The Times* (London). Results showed that *The New York Times* devoted nearly twice as many words to the war as *The Times* (London); the majority of the articles were neutral; *The New York Times* was more favourable to the leftist and was as favourable to the rightists as *The Times* (London); the two newspapers were consistent in direction, and all deviation from neutrality remained within the limits of mild intensity.

190.

Sinno, Abdul Karim. 1980. "Media Coverage of the Lebanese Civil War." Master's thesis, University of Wisconsin.

The author analysed 42 issues of the coverage of the Lebanese Civil War in *The New York Times* and *An-Nahar** (Lebanon) from April 1975 to September 1976. Content was measured according to four coding systems: (1) the religious terms with subcategories: Muslim, Christian and general; (2) religious/political associations with subcategories: Muslim-Left, Muslim-Right, Christian-Left and Christian-Right; (3) religious and political terms in sentences with subcategories: religious, political, political religious and descriptive; and (4) sentences with religious labels with subcategories: one religious label, more than one religious label and no labels. Results showed the two newspapers differed in the way they covered the war. The *Times* focused on the religious aspects of the war while the *An-Nahar* focused on political aspects. The *Times* coverage suggested the war was between Muslims and Christians while the *An-Nahar* suggested it was between different political parties. Emphasis of the *Times* associated Muslims with the Left and Christians with the Right and never vice versa.

* *An-Nahar* (The Day), founded in 1933, is a newspaper with a circulation of 85,000 in Lebanon.

191.

Havandjian, Nishan Rafi. 1979. "National Differences in the Press Coverage of the Lebanese War." Ph.D. dissertation, University of Texas.

The purpose of this study was to determine whether the press views foreign events through a socio-political value lens. The press (*Al-Ahram** of Egypt, *Le Monde* of France, and *The New York Times*) coverage of the Lebanese Civil War from April 1974 to December 1976 was analysed in three categories: straight news stories, interpretative articles incorporating news stories, interpretative articles incorporating news analysis and human interest stories, and signed and unsigned editorials. A composite list of socio-political values incorporating values from the three different cultures was devised. Results tended to support the major premise that the press views and interprets events in terms of the society it represents. While there were shared values among the papers, each of them stressed significantly different values. *Al-Ahram* emphasized group unity, nationalism, honour and sacrifice; *Le Monde* highlighted culture, civilization, freedom and friendship; and *The New York Times* stressed democracy and strength.

* *Al-Ahram* (The Pyramids) is an Arabic newspaper published in Cairo, Egypt. Its circulation is 900,000 for the weekday and 1.1 million for Friday.

192.

Kessler, Andjela Loncaric. 1979. "A Comparative Content Analysis: The Coverage of the Fifth Non-Aligned Conference by Associated Press and the Yugoslav News Agency Tanjug." Master's thesis, University of Georgia.

> This study compared the coverage of the Fifth Non-Aligned Conference, which was a significant Third World "media" event held in Colombo August 1976 between the AP and the Tanjug.* It was found that Tanjug devoted five times greater coverage than the AP and gave a more complete coverage than AP in matters concerning mutual interests among Non-Aligned countries. AP gave priority to news events about the changes in the Non-Aligned Movement that would have an impact on the Western world, particularly the U.S.

> * The full name of Tanjug is Novinska Agencija Tanjug. Founded in 1943, it has 90 correspondents in Yugoslavia and 50 offices abroad. It is a press and information agency governed by self-management, providing the following services: news service for the Yugoslavian press, radio and television; news and feature service for abroad in English, French, Spanish, Russian and German; features service in Arabic; photo and telephoto service; economic and financial service for home and abroad; publishes EITI, service for trade, industry, and banking in Serbo-Croat, English, French, German and Spanish; computerized commodity service for Yugoslav businesses and banks.

193.

Kook, Hee Yon. 1979. "A Comparative Content Anaylsis of Korean News in *The New York Times* and *The Washington Post*." Master's thesis, East Texas State University.

> The purpose of this study was to determine how Korean news was reported, how comprehensive the news was, and what the image of Korea was in *The New York Times* and *The Washington Post* from 1 July 1977 to 30 June 1978. It was found that the *Post* carried slightly more Korean news in terms of items, space and illustrations than the *Times*. In both papers, American sources outnumbered Korean sources. The *Post* had more opinions in news stories than the *Times* did in in-depth reporting. Both papers carried more negative than positive news, but the *Times* carried less negative news than the *Post*. In addition, the emphasis in Korean news was placed on hard news while human-interest stories and cultural activities were almost ignored.

194.

Leung, Wai-yin Kenneth. 1979. "News Flow Between the United States and Asia." Ph.D. dissertation, University of Minnesota.

Leung attempted to prove or disprove some of the Third World charges against the Western media by examining the process of news flow between the U.S. and Asia. He examined the UPI wire copies filed between the American continent and Asia during two seven-day periods in August 1977, simultaneously anaylsing the end use of the UPI wire stories and those of all other global agencies in six U.S. and six Asian newspapers.* Data confirmed the imbalance of news flow between the U.S. and Asia, with the amount of Asia-bound U.S. news about four times as much as the U.S.-bound Asian news. The author pointed out the fact that more and more Third World countries were establishing their own news agencies, which implies they are no longer passive recipients of information from the Western news agencies. The frequent allegation that the Western agencies are biased against the Third World countries are not too well-founded because more stories covered, written and disseminated by these agencies are "unfavourable" to the U.S. than to the Third World countries. Nevertheless, the author agreed that the Western agencies reported more sensational news of tension or violence than the development news about the Third World.

* The six U.S. newspapers are: *The New York Times*, *Los Angeles Times*, *St. Louis Post-Dispatch*, *Denver Post*, *St. Paul Dispatch* and *Arkansas Gazette*.

195.

Li, Ruey-feng Shieh. 1980. "Coverage of the Chinese-Vietnamese War (February 17, 1979 to March 5, 1979): American Newspapers versus Chinese Newspapers." Master's thesis, University of Georgia.

This study compared the coverage of the Chinese-Vietnamese War between two American newspapers (*The New York Times* and *Chicago Tribune*) and two Chinese newspapers (*World Journal* and *China Daily News*).* It was found that the two Chinese newspapers (one pro-Nationalist and the other pro-Communist) devoted more space to the coverage than the American newspapers. Both Chinese newspapers placed the news on more prominent pages than did the American newspapers. The Chinese newspapers relied most heavily on news agencies while the American newspapers on "unidentified" sources; the pro-Nationalist *World Journal* took a neutral stand on the coverage as the American newspapers did while the pro-Communist *China Daily News* reported the war very favourably to Communist China and unfavourably to Vietnam.

* *World Journal* is a Chinese-language newspaper published in New York by the Republic of China for the Chinese living in the U.S.A. *China Daily*, an English-language newspaper founded in 1981 in Beijing, covers China's political, economic and cultural developments as well as world financial and sports news. Its circulation is 150,000. It is also printed in Shanghai, Guangzhou, Xi'an, Hong Kong and New York.

196.

Wang, Wen-rang. 1979. "The Favorable and Unfavorable Attitudes of Segments of the American Press toward Communist China and the Republic of China before and after President Nixon's Visit to Peking in 1972." Master's thesis, Univesity of Georgia.

Wang examined the coverage of the People's Republic of China and the Republic of China from 1969 to 1975 in *The New York Times*, *Chicago Tribune* and *The Washington Post*. A favourable attitude toward the PRC was found from 1971 to 1973, but from 1974 to 1975 the favourable percentages dropped almost to the same level of those in 1969 and 1970 probably due to the slowdown of the process of Sino-American normalization. The author also found the political stance of each paper was related to its favourable or unfavourable coverage of the PRC.

197.

Ayanru, Osagie E. 1978. "A Content Analysis of the Coverage of the Angolan Civil War by *Newsweek* and *Time* Magazine." Master's thesis, West Virginia Univesity.

This study attempted to discover whether the attributed and unattributed opinion, inference and judgement sentences used by *Newsweek* and *Time* in their coverage of the Angolan Civil War were favourable or unfavourable to either the Popular Movement for the Liberation of Angola

(PMLA) or National Front for the Liberation of Angola (NFLA)/ National Union for the Total Independence of Angola (NUTIA). The sentence was the coding unit. A set of nine categories was devised: reports, attributed reports; opinions, attributed opinions; inferences, attributed inferences; judgements, attributed judgements; and all others. The study found the two magazines reported events related to the Angolan Civil War consistently. There was no bias for or against either faction as the opinion, inference and judgement sentences were backed by a considerable amount of factual sentences.

198.

Kam, Margaret L. 1978. "A Comparative Study of the Chinese News Coverage in *The New York Times* and the U.S. Coverage in the *People's Daily* during Three Selected Periods." Master's thesis, San Jose State University.

This study examined how *The New York Times* and *People's Daily* covered news in each other's country over three periods: April 1966, April 1971 and April 1976 (i.e. before, during and after the "Ping-pong" diplomacy of 1971). Two questions were asked: (1) What have the newspapers reported about the other's country during these periods? (2) Was there any measureable change in the volume of news and in press attitude of either one or both countries since the friendlier relations of 1971? The news source, geographical origin and direction were analysed. Twelve subject-matter categories were used to classify the news content. Two hypotheses were supported: (1) The amount of news published in the two newspapers would be dependent on the kinds of governmental relations which each country held to the other country during any period studied. (2) The favourable or unfavourable coverage of the two newspapers would directly or indirectly reflect the political interests and concerns of the governments of the two countries toward each other during each stage of their relationship. As expected, *The New York Times*' coverage of China became more favourable as governmental relations improved after the "Ping-pong" diplomacy of 1971. In the case of *People's Daily*, its U.S. coverage decreased rather than increased after the Vietnam War. Also, the newspaper decreased its hostility toward the U.S, but Kam says it was more a result of the termination of the

Indo-China War than a consequence of the improved diplomatic relations.

199.

Adophy, Michael Obi Simon. 1977. "A Comparative Study of Nigerian News in *Newsweek* and *Time*, 1960 to 1976." Master's thesis, East Texas State University.

> This study intended to find how *Newsweek* and *Time* reported Nigerian news from 1960 to 1976. It was found that both magazines gave Nigeria adequate coverage during the period studied, but the coverage was largely crisis-oriented—political and social disorder, military coups and civil war were given extensive coverage. The author also included a questionnaire survey of Nigerian students in the U.S. who indicated that Nigeria needs well-trained journalists and a Nigerian-owned news agency.

200.

Kishfy, Nancy. 1977. "Chilean Coverage, 1960–1965–1971, by Three U.S. Dailies." Master's thesis, California State Univesity at Northridge.

> This study examined the coverage of Chile by *The Washington Post*, the *Chicago Tribune*, and the *Los Angeles Times* quantitatively and qualitatively in 1960, 1965 and 1971. Articles about Chile were broken down into headline, lead and body. Each was analysed separately. The theme was classified as political, economic or social; the direction of the headline, lead and body were categorized as violent, non-violent, or neutral. It was found that there were mainly short articles about Chile; mostly wire services were used as a source. Leads of the articles tended to be more violent than headlines and body of the articles. In the three years violent news dominated; though the papers all improved their coverage in terms of amount and variety of topics in 1971 compared to 1965 and 1960, violent news about Chile was reported at the expense of other political, social and economical issues.

201.

Atoyebi, Atilade O. 1976. "Coverage of Southern Africa in Four

Newspapers from the U.S., Britain, and Kenya: 1974–75." Master's thesis, University of Wisconsin.

This thesis examines the coverage of the political developments in Southern Africa by *The Washington Post*, *The Times* (London), *The Gazette* (Canada), and *Daily Nation** (Kenya). The content of the newspapers was analysed to compare the frequency and the amount of space devoted to African issues, the relative impact of the Southern African situation on the newspapers' coverage of Africa, the aspect of the political crisis emphasized by each newspaper and the extent to which national foreign policies were reflected in the newspapers' editorial opinions. It was found that *The Times* more frequently reported African issues than either *The Washington Post* or *The Gazette*. The political crisis in Southern Africa received more attention in the newspapers than any other issues. The thesis also indicated a positive relationship between the newspapers' editorial opinions on the crisis and their respective governments' official policies concerning the crisis.

* *Daily Nation*, founded in 1960, is an English newspaper with a circulation of 165,000 in Nairobi, Kenya.

202.

Marcus, Beverly S. 1976. "The Changing Image of the Palestinians in Three U.S. Publications: 1948–74." Master's thesis, University of Wisconsin.

Since 1948, four major wars have been fought between Israel and her Arab neighbours, resulting in thousands of Palestinian refugees. This study examined how *The New York Times*, *Chicago Tribune*, and *Time* magazine portrayed the Palestinian people and problem from 1948–1974. It was found that the Palestinians were either ignored by the press or portrayed as anonymous, passive, helpless Arab refugees until 1967, when they initiated their campaign of spectacular international terrorism. Though giving Palestinian terrorism massive play, the publications studied provided little information on the history and complexities of the Palestinian dilemma. It was only with the 1973 war and Arab oil boycott that the press began to treat Palestinian national aspirations seriously. In addition, the study discussed the causes of that portrayal such as the judgements about the Palestinian newsworthiness, and pro-Israeli and anti-Arab bias.

203.

Sudhaker, Anantha B. 1976. "The Bangladesh War in Print: An Analysis of Three American and Three Indian English Language Newspapers' Coverage." Master's thesis, University of Oklahoma.

This study content analysed the performance of *The New York Times*, *The Washington Post*, *Los Angeles Times*, *The Times of India*, *The Hindu* and *Hindustan Time** during the Indo-Pakistan War in 1971 resulting in the birth of Bangladesh. It dealt with the volume of reporting on the front page and the amount of editorial attention given to the event during the period from 1 November 1971 to 31 December 1971. The editorial tone of these papers—positive, negative and neutral—is also measured. Analyses included percentage of space devoted to the event in column inches, daily percentage of editorials on the issue and its space and the sources of information. These questions were asked: How does the pattern of coverage of the event vary in the Indian and American newspapers? If the national interest is involved, do the media operate in a different manner and assume social responsibility? If yes, how do the media fulfill their task? Does proximity to such an event of global magnitude affect Indian newspapers? If yes, to what extent? And to what extent does the press coverage in these two countries differ? It was found that editorial attention and reporting frequently fluctuated considerably among the American newspapers. There was a significant difference between Indian and American newspapers concerning the volume of reporting and the number of editorials on the topic. But no difference was found between the number of editorials as the tone was concerned.

* These three newspapers are Indian publications. *The Times of India*, founded in 1838, is an English morning newspaper published in Bombay. It also publishes from Delhi, Ahmadabad, Bangalore, Jaipur, Patna and Lucknow. Its circulation (Bombay and Bangalore) is 297,000. *The Hindu*, founded in 1878, is an independent English morning newspaper in Madras. It also publishes from Bangalore, Coimbatore, Hyderabad, New Delhi and Madurai. The combined circulation of *The Hindu* is around 418,000. *The Hindustan Times*, founded in 1923, is an English morning newspaper in New Delhi. Its circulation in Delhi is 268,000.

Appendices

I. Selected Western Newspapers

The first column of circulation figure is for morning papers and the second column is for Sunday papers unless otherwise specified: (E) = Evening; (S) = Saturday; (A) = Afternoon; (MF) = Monday Through Friday; (W) = Wednesday; (Wk) = Weekly; (T) = Tuesday; (Th) = Thursday; (F) = Friday; (D) = All Day; N.A. = Not Available. The sign "†" indicates the world's great dailies according to *The World's Great Dailies: Profiles of Fifty Newspapers* written by John C. Merrill and Harold A. Fisher (1980).

Sources: *The Europa International Yearbook* (1989) and *World Press Encyclopedia* (1982).

U.S.A.*

	Year Founded	Circulation	Circulation
Alabama			
Birmingham News	1888	169,000 (E)	211,000
Alaska			
Anchorage News	1946	56,000	68,000
Arizona			
Arizona Republic	1890	343,000	539,000
Arkansas			
Arkansas Gazette	1819	137,000	185,000
California			
Los Angeles Times†	1881	1,118,000 (D)	1,397,000
San Francisco Chronicle	1865	558,000	—
San Francisco Examiner	1865	142,000 (E)	—
Colorado			
Rocky Mountain News	1859	348,000	380,000
Connecticut			
Hartford Courant	1764	225,000	309,000
Delaware			
Journal	1871	51,000 (E)	—
News	1880	67,000	—
News Journal	1975	—	132,000
District of Columbia			
USA Today	1982	1,467,000	—
Washington Post†	1877	796,000	1,113,000

* The newspaper with the largest circulation in each of the 50 U.S. states is included.

	Year Founded	Circulation	Circulation
Florida			
The Miami Herald[†]	1910	437,000	546,000
St. Petersburg Times	1906	308,000	395,000
Georgia			
The Atlanta Constitution[†]	1868	265,000	—
Atlanta Journal-Constitution (S)	N.A.	—	646,000
Hawaii			
Honolulu Advertiser	1856	85,000	—
Honolulu Star-Bulletin	1912	100,000 (E)	—
Honolulu Star-Bulletin &	1962	—	196,000
Advertiser			
Idaho			
Idaho Statesman	1864	55,000	70,000
Illinois			
Chicago Sun and Times	1948	758,000	626,000
Chicago Tribune	1847	758,000	1,126,000
Indiana			
Indianapolis Star	1903	230,000	400,000
Iowa			
Des Moines Register	1849	222,000	365,000
Kansas			
Witchita Eagle-Beacon	1872	129,000	194,000
Kentucky			
Courier Journal[†]	1868	267,000	323,000
Louisiana			
New Orleans Times-Picayune	1880	281,000 (D)	352,000
Maine			
Bangor News	1834	78,000	94,000
Maryland			
Baltimore Sun[†]	1837	223,000	490,000
Massachusettes			
The Boston Globe	1872	500,000	798,000
The Christian Science Monitor[†]	1908	186,000	—
Michigan			
Detroit Free Press	1831	640,000	724,000
Detroit News	1873	677,000 (D)	838,000
Minnesota			
Star Tribune	1867	383,000 (D)	626,000

	Year Founded	Circulation	Circulation
Mississippi			
Clarion-Ledger	1837	68,000	115,000
Missouri			
St. Louis Post-Dispatch[†]	1878	357,000	549,000
Montana			
Billings Gazette	1885	58,000	60,000
Nebraska			
Omaha World Herald	1885	120,000	290,000
Nevada			
Las Vegas Review-Journal	1908	114,000 (D)	135,000
New Hampshire			
Union Leader	1946	69,000	—
New Jersey			
Star-Ledger	1917	461,000	682,000
New Mexico			
Albuquerque Journal	1880	105,000	143,000
New York			
The Buffalo News	1880	378,000 (D)	311,000
New York City			
New York Daily News	1919	1,278,000	1,632,000
New York Post	1801	740,000	—
The New York Times[†]	1851	1,057,000	1,645,000
The Wall Street Journal[†]	1889	2,026,000	—
North Carolina			
Charlotte Observer	1886	219,000	275,000
North Dakota			
The Forum	1878	55,000	68,000
Ohio			
Cleveland Plain Dealer	1842	452,000	430,000
Oklahoma			
Oklahoman	1894	233,000	328,000
Oregon			
The Oregonian	1850	322,000	404,000
Pennsylvania			
Philadelphia Inquirer	1829	495,000	989,000
Rhode Island			
Providence Journal	1829	97,000	262,000
South Carolina			
The State	1891	136,000	—

	Year Founded	Circulation	Circulation
South Dakota			
Argus Leader	1881	45,000	65,000
Tennessee			
The Commercial Appeal	1840	224,000	291,000
Texas			
Austin American-Statesman	1871	167,000 (D)	205,000
Dallas Morning News	1885	391,000	531,000
Dallas Times Herald	1876	246,000 (D)	339,000
Fort Worth Star Telegram	1895	136,000	319,000
Houston Chronicle	1901	406,000 (D)	532,000
Houston Post	1885	315,000	366,000
Utah			
Salt Lake City Tribune	1871	113,000	143,000
Vermont			
The Free Press	1896	49,000	54,000
Virginia			
Virginian-Pilot	1865	144,000	227,000
Washington			
Seattle Post-Intelligencer	1863	204,000	501,000
West Virginia			
Charleston Gazette	1873	54,000	109,000
Wisconsin			
Milwaukee Journal	1882	289,000 (E)	517,000
Milwaukee Sentinel	1837	196,000	—
Wyoming			
Star-Tribune	1914	35,000	40,000

Canada*

	Year Founded	Circulation	Circulation
Alberta			
Calgary Herald	1883	138,000	124,000
Edmonton Journal	1903	169,000	149,000
British Columbia			
Times-Colonist (Victoria)	1858	81,000	78,000
The Vancouver Sun	1886	227,000 (E)	—

* The newspaper with the largest circulation in each of the Canadian provinces is
included.

	Year Founded	Circulation	Circulation
Manitoba			
Winnipeg Free Press[†]	1874	179,000 (E)	146,000
New Brunswick			
Daily Gleaner (Fredericton)	1880	29,000 (E)	—
Telegraph-Journal and Evening Times-Globe	N.A.	63,000 (D)	—
Newfoundland			
Telegram (St. John's)	1879	39,000 (E)	55,000 (S)
Nova Scotia			
Chronicle-Herald (Halifax)	N.A.	87,000	—
Mail-Star (Halifax)	—	—	60,000 (E)
Ontario			
Le Droit	1913	39,000 (E)	—
The Globe and Mail[†]	1844	326,000	—
Hamilton Spectator	1846	144,000 (E)	—
London Free Press	1849	131,000	—
Ottawa Citizen	1843	192,000	249,000 (S)
Toronto Star	1892	519,000 (D)	533,000
		—	806,000 (S)
Toronto Sun	1971	290,000	461,000
Windsor Star	1918	88,000 (E)	—
Prince Edward Island			
Guardian and Patriot (Charlottetown)	1887	24,000 (D)	—
Quebec			
The Gazette	1778	192,000	272,000 (S)
La Presse	1884	207,000	184,000
		—	327,000 (S)
Le Journal de Montréal	1964	328,000	348,000
		—	355,000 (S)
Le Soleil	1896	115,000	94,000
		—	145,000 (S)
Saskatchewan			
Leader-Post (Regina)	1883	72,000 (E)	—
Yukon Territory			
Whitehorse Star	1985	3,000	—

Australia*

	Year Founded	Circulation
Australian Capital Territory		
The Canberra Times	1926	44,000
New South Wales		
The Australian	1964	138,000
Daily Mirror	1941	395,000
Daily Telegraph[†]	1879	326,000
Sun-Herald	1953	671,000 (Wk)
Sunday Telegraph	1938	665,000 (Wk)
The Sydney Morning Herald[†]	1831	400,000 (S)
Northern Territory		
Northern Territory News	1952	19,000
Queensland		
Courier Mail	1933	257,000
Sunday Mail	1923	320,000 (Wk)
Sunday Sun	1971	371,000 (Wk)
South Australia		
Advertiser	1858	216,000
Sunday Mail	1912	250,000 (Wk)
Tasmania		
Mercury	1854	58,000
The Tasmanian Mail	1978	131,000 (Wk)
Victoria		
The Age[†]	1854	236,000
The Herald	1840	217,000
Sun News-Pictorial	1922	570,000
Sunday Observer	1971	135,000 (Wk)
Truth	1890	210,000 (Wk)
Western Australia		
Daily News	1882	100,000
Sunday Times	1897	280,000 (Wk)
The West Australia	1833	281,000

* The newspaper with the largest circulation in each of the states and territories is selected.

United Kingdom

	Year Founded	Circulation	Circulation
London			
Daily Express	1900	1,679,438	—
Daily Mail	1896	1,792,701	—
Daily Mirror	1903	3,082,215	—
Daily Star	1978	1,013,688	—
Daily Telegraph	1771	1,138,673	—
Evening Standard	1827	522,407 (E)	—
Financial Times	1880	286,774	—
The Guardian[†]	1821	470,023	—
The Independent	1986	375,317	—
The Observer	1791	—	749,644 (Wk)
The Sun	1921	4,146,644	—
Sunday Express	1918	—	2,143,374 (Wk)
Sunday Mirror	1915	—	2,778,935 (Wk)
Sunday People	1881	—	2,932,472 (Wk)
Sunday Telegraph	1961	—	716,044 (Wk)
The Sunday Times	1822	—	1,314,504 (Wk)
The Times[†]	1785	450,626	—
Today	1986	408,078	—
Principal Provincial Dailies*			
Aberdeen			
Press and Journal	1748	110,784	—
Birmingham			
Birmingham Post	1857	N.A.	—
Sunday Mercury	1918	—	160,297 (Wk)
Brighton			
Evening Argus	1880	100,000 (E)	—
Bristol			
Evening Post	1932	109,790 (MF)	92,317 (S)
Cardiff			
South Wales Echo	1884	103,126 (E)	—
Coventry			
Coventry Evening Telegraph	1891	92,817 (MF)	113,449 (S)

* Provincial newspapers with circulation of 100,000 or more and leading newspapers
  with slightly lower circulation are selected.

	Year Founded	Circulation	Circulation
Dundee			
Courier and Advertiser	1810	128,061	—
Weekly News (Thomson's)	1855	—	670,502 (S)
Edinburgh			
Evening News	1873	127,675	—
Glasgow			
Daily Record	1895	758,921	—
Evening Times	N.A.	192,561	—
Glasgow Herald	1783	122,238	—
Scottish Daily Express	N.A.	155,000	—
Sunday Mail	N.A.	—	886,632 (Wk)
Sunday Post	1920	—	1,432,645 (Wk)
Kingston-upon-Hull			
Hull Daily Mail	1885	110,505 (E)	—
Leeds			
Yorkshire Evening Post	1890	149,405 (MF)	134,879 (S)
Yorkshire Post[†]	1754	92,374	—
Leicester			
Leicester Mercury	1874	151,000 (E)	—
Liverpool			
Liverpool Echo	1879	213,238 (E)	—
Manchester			
Manchester Evening News	1868	320,000 (E)	—
The Star	1978	1,136,840	—
Newcastle-upon-Tyne			
Evening Chronicle	1885	147,691 (MF)	133,941 (S)
The Sunday Sun	1919	—	126,743 (Wk)
Northern Ireland			
Belfast Telegraph	1870	150,000 (E)	—
Irish News	1855	43,000	—
Nottingham			
Nottingham Evening Post	1878	133,190 (E)	—
Sheffield			
The Star	1887	140,683 (MF)	143,331 (S)
Stoke-on-Trent			
Evening Sentinel	1873	107,502 (E)	—
West Bromwich			
Sandwell Evening Mail	1975	284,047 (E)	—

	Year Founded	Circulation	Circulation
Wolverhampton			
Express and Star	1975	339,273 (E)	—

France

	Year Founded	Circulation	Circulation
Paris Dailies			
Le Figaro	1828	433,496	—
France-Dimanche	N.A.	—	721,000
France Soir	1944	410,679	—
International Herald Tribune	1887	174,200	—
L'Humanité-Dimanche	1946	—	360,000
Libération	1973	165,539	—
Le Monde†	1944	362,443	—
Le Parisien Libere	1944	339,271	—
Le Quotidien de Paris	1974	75,000	—
Provincial Dailies*			
Angers			
Le Courrier de l'Ouest	1944	107,431	—
Bordeaux			
Sud-Quest	1944	356,989	—
Clermont-Ferrand			
La Montagne (Centre-France)	1919	252,457	—
Grenoble			
Le Dauphiné Libéré	1944	360,000	—
Lille			
La Voix du Nord	1944	377,219	—
Lyon			
Le Progrès	1859	453,600	—
Marseilles			
La Marseillaise	1944	159,039	—
Le Provencal	1944	178,502	—
Metz			
Le Républicain Lorrain	1919	214,280	—
Montpellier			
Midi Libre	1944	189,283	—

* Provincial newspapers with circulation of 100,000 or more are selected.

	Year Founded	Circulation	Circulation
Morlaix			
Le Télégramme de Brest et de l'Ouest	1944	201,963 (1985)	—
Mulhouse			
L'Alsace	1944	136,297	—
Nancy			
L'Est Républicain	1889	267,588	—
Nice			
Nice-Matin	1944	261,980	—
Reims			
L'Union	1944	117,812	—
Rennes			
Quest-France	1944	803,701 (1985)	—
Roubaix			
Nord Eclair	1944	102,773	—
Rouen			
Paris-Normandie	1944	129,030	—
Saint-Étienne			
La Tribune–Le Progrés	N.A.	130,000	—
Strasbourg			
Dernières Nouvelles d'Alsace	1877	220,082	—
Toulouse			
Dépêche du Midi	1870	247,533	—
Tours			
La Nouvelle République du Centre Ouest	1944	271,504 (1987)	—

Federal Republic of Germany (West Germany)*

	Year Founded	Circulation	Circulation
Augsburg			
Augsburger Allgemeine	N.A.	350,000	—
Berlin			
BZ (Berliner Zeitung)	1877	296,300	—
Bielefeld			
Neue Westfälische	1967	227,000	—

* Newspapers with circulation of 200,000 or more are selected.

	Year Founded	Circulation	Circulation
Bonn			
Die Welt[†]	1946	225,000	—
Cologne			
Express	1964	447,500	—
Kölner Stadt-Anzeiger	1876	265,800	—
Dortmund			
Ruhr Nachrichten	1949	269,000	—
Westfälische Rundschau	N.A.	250,000	—
Düsseldorf			
Rheinische Post	1946	401,000	—
Westdeutsche Zeitung	N.A.	200,000	—
Essen			
Neue Ruhr-Zeitung	N.A.	215,000	—
Westdeutsche Allgemeine Zeitung	N.A.	660,000	—
Frankfurt am Main			
Frankfurter Allgemeine Zeitung[†]	1949	360,000	—
Frankfurter Rundschau	N.A.	196,000	—
Hamburg			
Bild am Sonntag	1956	—	2,400,000
Bild Zeitung	1952	5,124,000	—
Die Zeit	1946	468,000 (W)	—
Hamburger Abendblatt	N.A.	280,000	358,000 (S)
Welt am Sonntag	N.A.	—	336,000
Hanover			
Hannoversche Allgemeine Zeitung	N.A.	220,000	—
Kassel			
Hessische/Niedersächsische Allgemeine	1959	230,000	—
Koblenz			
Rhein-Zeitung	N.A.	233,000	—
Leutkirch			
Schwäbische Zeitung	1945	202,000	—
Ludwigshafen			
Die Rheinpfalz	N.A.	250,000	—
Munich			
Süddeutsche Zeitung[†]	1945	378,420	—

	Year Founded	Circulation	Circulation
Abend Zeitung/8-Uhr-Blatt	1948	260,000	—
Münster			
Westfälische Nachrichten	N.A.	215,000	—
Nuremberg			
Nürnberger Nachrichten	1945	336,175	—
Osnabrück			
Neue Osnabrücker Zeitung	1967	289,508	—
Saarbrücken			
Saarbrücker Zeitung	1761	205,000	—
Stuttgart			
Stuttgarter Nachrichten	1946	260,000	—
Stuttgarter Zeitung	N.A.	503,925	—
Ulm			
Südwest Presse	N.A.	361,924	—

The German Democratic Republic (East Germany)*

	Year Founded	Circulation
Berlin		
Berliner Zeitung	1945	424,949
Berliner Zeitung (BZ) am Abend	N.A.	203,653 (E)
Junge Welt	1947	1,380,477
Neues Deutschland	1946	1,092,811
Tribune	1945	414,200
Cottbus		
Lausitzer Rundschau	N.A.	291,073
Dresden		
Sächsische Zeitung	1946	560,800
Frankfurt an der Oder		
Neuer Tag	N.A.	210,507
Gera		
Volkswacht	N.A.	237,537
Halle		
Freiheit	1946	584,505
Karl-Marx-Stadt		
Freie Presse	N.A.	660,945

* Newspapers with circulation of 200,000 or more and leading provincial newspapers with slightly lower circulation are selected.

	Year Founded	Circulation
Leipzig		
Leipziger Volkszeitung	1894	485,000
Magdeburg		
Freie Erde	1945	201,461
Volksstimme	N.A.	450,685
Potsdam		
Markische Volksstimme	N.A.	347,495
Rostock		
Ostsee Zeitung	1952	292,469
Schwerin		
Schweriner Volkszeitung	1946	201,299
Suhl		
Freies Wort	N.A.	177,460

Denmark*

	Year Founded	Circulation	Circulation
Aabenraa			
Jydske Tidende	N.A.	38,064	53,689
Alborg			
Aalborg Stiftstidende (E)	1767	73,964	100,496
Arhus			
Aarhuus Stiftstidende (E)	1794	70,862	89,098
Den Blä Avis (Th)	N.A.	55,500	—
Copenhagen			
Berlingske Tidende[†]	1749	128,815	165,341
B.T.	1916	202,750	171,679
Det Fri Aktuelt	1871	66,661	79,484
Ekstra Bladet (E)	1904	229,509	175,960
Erhvervs-Bladet	N.A.	104,386	—
Politiken	1884	152,215	186,391
Esbjerg			
Vestkysten (E)	1917	55,766	—
Hillerød			
De Bergske Blade	N.A.	109,230	—
Viby			
Jyllands-Posten, Morgenavisen	N.A.	128,600	215,231

* Newspapers with circulation of 50,000 or more are selected.

The Netherlands*

	Year Founded	Circulation
Alkmaar		
Noordhollands Dagblad	1799	134,600
Amsterdam		
Het Parool	1945	113,600 (E)
Del Telegraaf	1893	706,000
Trouw	1943	122,600
De Volkskrant	1919	310,000
Breda		
De Stem	1860	107,795
Enschede		
Dagblad Tubantia	1872	102,594
Groningen		
Nieuwsblad van het Noorden	1888	136,800 (E)
Houten		
Utrechts Nieuwsblad	1893	101,256 (E)
Leeuwarden		
Leeuwarder Courant	1752	110,573 (E)
Maastricht		
De Limburger	1845	137,126
Nijmegen		
De Gelderlander	1848	165,702
Rijswijk/The Hague		
Haagsche Courant	1883	178,102 (E)
(incl. *Het Binnenhof*)		
Rotterdam		
Algemeen Dagblad	1946	417,000
NRC Handelsblad	1970	215,000 (E)
Rotterdams Nieuwsblad	1878	181,925 (E)
(incl. *Het Vrije Volk*)		

* Newspapers with circulation of 100,000 or more are selected.

Belgium*

	Year Founded	Circulation
Antwerp		
Gazet van Antwerpen (with *Gazet van Mechelen*)	1891	189,971
De Nieuwe Gazet (with *Het Laastste Nieuwe*)	1897	301,306
Brussels		
Het Laatste Nieuws (with *De Nieuwe Gazet*)	1888	301,306 (Dutch)
La Bibre Belgique	1884	80,818
La Dernière Heure (with *Les Sports*)	1906	95,000
La Lanterne (with *La Meuse*)	1944	132,844 (Dutch)
De Nieuwe Gids (with *Het Volk*)	1944	189,513
Le Soir	1887	208,833
Krantengroep De Standaard (Group combining *De Standaard*, *Het Nieuwsblad, De Gentenaar*)	N.A.	378,697
Ghent		
Het Volk (with *De Nieuwe Gids*)	1891	189,531
Hasselt		
Het Belang Van Limburg	1879	99,027
Liège		
La Meuse (with *La Lanterne*)	1855	132,844
Mechelen		
Gazet van Mechelen (with *Gazet van Antwerpen*)	1896	189,971

* Newspapers with circulation of 80,000 or more are selected.

New Zealand*

	Year Founded	Circulation	Circulation
Auckland Star (E)	1870	111,001 (MF)	160,000
The Dominion	1907	76,000	—
The Dominion Sunday Times	1981	—	88,000
Evening Post	1865	83,000	—
New Zealand Herald	1863	239,337	—

* Newspapers with circulation of 50,000 or more are selected.

	Year Founded	Circulation	Circulation
New Zealand Truth (Wk)	1905	125,000 (T)	—
Otago Daily Times	1861	52,000	—
The Press	1861	88,400	—
The Star (E)	1868	58,000	—

Finland*

	Year Founded	Circulation	Circulation
Helsinki			
Helsingin Sanomat[†]	1889	453,597	538,370
Kansan Uutiset	1957	45,731	57,262
Uusi Suomi	1847	154,794	96,457
Kuopio			
Savon Sanomat	1907	84,712	—
Tampere			
Aamulehti	1881	141,896	148,215

* Newspapers with circulation of 50,000 or more are selected.

Switzerland*

	Year Founded	Circulation	Circulation
Basel			
Basler Zeitung	1977	114,413	—
Berne			
Berner Zeitung	1844	121,887	—
Der Bund	1850	62,326	—
Geneva			
Journal de Genève	1826	22,254	—
La Suisse	1898	70,032	110,522
Tribune de Genève (A)	1879	63,734	—
Lausanne			
24 heures	1762	96,851	—
Lucerne (Luzern)			
Luzerner Neueste Nachrichten	1896	57,290	—
Vaterland	N.A.	51,217	—
St Gallen (St Gall)			
St Gallen Tagblatt	1839	53,000	—

* Newspapers with circulation of 50,000 or more are selected.

	Year Founded	Circulation	Circulation
Zürich			
Blick	N.A.	382,275	—
Neue Zürcher Zeitung[†]	1780	145,735	—
Tages Anzeiger Zurich	1893	256,767	—

II. Principal International News Agencies

Sources: *The Europa International Yearbook* (1989) and *World Press Encyclopedia* (1982).

Agence France-Presse (AFP) (Paris, France):
  founded 1914; 24-hour service of world political, financial, sporting news and photographs; 150 agencies and 2,000 correspondents all over the world.

Associated Press (AP) (New York, USA):
  founded 1848; 1,697 newspaper members in the U.S., 6,000 broadcast members and over 8,500 subscribers abroad.

Deutsche Presse-Agentur (DPA) (Hamburg, West Germany):
  founded in 1949; supplies all the daily newspapers, broadcasting stations and some 1,000 further subscribers in the Federal Republic of Germany and West Berlin with its national and regional news service. English, Spanish, Arabic and German language news is also transmitted regularly to 550 press agencies, newspapers, radio and television stations and ministries of information in over 85 countries.

Reuters Holdings PLC (Reuters) (London, UK):
  founded 1851; world-wide news and information service by computer and teleprinter to business clients in 133 countries and media clients in 158 countries.

Telegrafnoye Agentstvo Sovetskovo Soyuza (Telegraphic Agency of the Soviet Union) (TASS) (Moscow, USSR):
  founded 1925; serves 4,000 Soviet newspapers and 550 foreign press agencies in 110 countries.

United Press International (UPI) (Washington, D.C., USA):
  founded 1907; serves 8,000 news outlets world-wide.

Xinhua (New China) News Agency (NCNA) (Beijing, PRC):
  founded in 1931; offices in all Chinese provincial capitals, and about 95 overseas bureaux; news service in Chinese, English, French, Spanish, Arabic and Russian, feature and photographic services.

III. List of Third World Countries and Territories

Sources: *The Times Family Atlas of the World*. First edition. Mass.: Salem House Publishers, 1989.

Afghanistan

Albania

Algeria

Andorra

Angola

Antigua and Barbuda

Argentina

Bahamas

Bahrain

Bangladesh

Barbados

Belize

Benin

Bermuda

Bhutan

Bolivia

Botswana

Brazil

Brunei

Burkina

Burma

Burundi

Cambodia

Cameroon

Cape Verde

Central African Republic

Chad

Chile

China, People's Republic of

Colombia

Comoros

Congo

Cook Islands[†] (New Zealand)

Costa Rica

Cuba

Cyprus

Djibouti

Dominica

Dominican Republic

Ecuador

Egypt

El Salvador

Equatorial Guinea

Ethiopia

Falkland Islands[†] (UK)

Fiji

French Guiana[†] (France)

French Polynesia[†] (France)

Gabon

Gambia

Ghana

Gibraltar[†] (UK)

Grenada

Guadeloupe[†] (France)

Guatemala

Guinea

[†] Indicates territory associated with the country in parentheses.

Guinea-Bissau
Guyana
Haiti
Honduras
Hong Kong[†] (UK)
India
Indonesia
Iran
Iraq
Ivory Coast
Jamaica
Jordan
Kenya
Kiribati
Korea, North
Korea, South
Kuwait
Laos
Lebanon
Lesotho
Liberia
Libya
Macau[†] (Portugal)
Madagascar
Malawi
Malaysia
Maldives
Mali
Malta
Martinique[†] (France)
Mauritania
Mauritius
Mexico
Mongolia
Morocco
Mozambique
Namibia

Nauru
Nepal
Netherlands Antilles[†]
  (Netherlands)
New Caledonia[†] (France)
Nicaragua
Niger
Nigeria
Oman
Pakistan
Palestine
Panama
Papua New Guinea
Paraguay
Peru
Philippines
Portugal
Qatar
Réunion[†] (France)
Rwanda
San Marino
Sao Tome and Principe
Saudi Arabia
Senegal
Seychelles
Sierra Leone
Singapore
Solomon Islands
Somalia
Sri Lanka
St. Kitts-Nevis
St. Lucia
St. Vincent
Sudan
Surinam
Swaziland
Syria

Taiwan[†] (Republic of China)

Tanzania

Thailand

Togo

Tonga

Trinidad and Tobago

Tunisia

Turkey

Tuvalu

Uganda

United Arab Emirates

Uruguay

Vanuatu

Vatican City

Venezuela

Virgin Islands[†] (UK)

Virgin Islands[†] (USA)

Vietnam

Wallis and Futuna Islands[†]
  (France)

Western Samoa

Wrangel Islands[†] (USSR)

Yemen

Yugoslavia

Zaire

Zambia

Zimbabwe

Index of Content Analysis*

Newspapers and Magazines

* Index by entry number.

News Agencies

Author Index[*]

* Index by entry number.

Subject Index*

A

Aamulehti, 27

Accountability, 185. *See also*
  Responsibilities

Accuracy, 50, 73, 83, 136, 144, 172. *See
  also* Bias

Actuel Developpement, 4

Afghanistan, 26, 85

Africa, 4, 12, 17, 24, 25, 36, 41, 42, 45,
  48, 64, 67, 72, 77, 79, 86, 89, 127, 128,
  136, 153, 165, 176, 177, 179, 201

Agence France-Presse (AFP), 64, 68, 89,
  107, 116, 128, 146, 149

Agenda diversity, 104

Al-Ahram, 191

Al-Doumhouria, 187

Algeria(n), 126, 187

Alternative
  model of international news, 183
  New World Information Order
    (NWIO), 107
  news services, 55
  sources, 65, 130

America(n), 1, 3, 12, 13, 22, 24, 30, 36,
  46, 61, 77, 78, 79, 80, 81, 85, 87, 88,
  89, 91, 93, 95, 99, 103, 104, 109, 120,
  128, 129, 130, 131, 132, 135, 136, 137,
  138, 144, 151, 155, 156, 172, 175, 176,
  179, 180, 184, 185, 186, 193, 203. *See
  also* U.S.
  Central, 3, 22, 127, 136
  Latin/South, 4, 12, 13, 33, 55, 63, 89,
    95, 101, 110, 116, 128, 145, 180, 184
  North, 13, 110, 127, 130, 138, 139,
    144, 156

American Broadcasting Company
  (ABC), 8, 184

American Newspaper Publishers
  Association (ANPA), 78

American Society of Newspaper Editors
  (ASNE), 36

An-Nahar, 190

Ang Pahayagang Malaya, 104

Angola(n), 86, 165
  Civil War, 197

Arab News, 105

Arab-Israeli conflict, 91, 169

Arab(s)/Arabic, 1, 91, 94, 105, 150, 151,
  169, 175, 186, 191, 202

Argentina/Argentinian, 13, 116

Arkansas Gazette, 194

Asia(n), 9, 16, 19, 21, 24, 26, 34, 42, 43,
  59, 76, 89, 109, 127, 146, 158, 160,
  194

Associated Press, The (AP), 18, 24, 25,
  39, 60, 68, 69, 75, 89, 107, 116, 128,
  136, 146, 149, 168, 192

Association of Southeast Asian Nations
  (ASEAN), 43, 50

Atlanta Constitution, The, 5, 88, 177

Atlanta Daily World, 177

Attention, 12, 24, 29, 34, 35, 38, 47, 70,
  91, 100, 111, 112, 139, 149, 161, 167,
  178, 179, 201, 203
  map, 70
  scores, 161, 178

Attributed/attribution(s), 1, 37, 94, 116,
  186
  inferences, 197
  judgements, 197

* Index by entry number.